Working with Parents as
Partners in SEN

'n below.

Working with Parents as Partners in SEN

Eileen Gascoigne

David Fulton Publishers

London

David Fulton Publishers Ltd
2 Barbon Close, London WC1N 3JX

First published in Great Britain by David Fulton Publishers 1995

Reprinted 1996

British Library Cataloguing in Publication Data

A catalogue record for this book is available from the British Library

ISBN 1-85346-375-2

Typeset by The Harrington Consultancy
Printed in Great Britain by the Cromwell Press Ltd., Melksham

Contents

It is the parents'
unreasonable commitment
to their child
that makes them
good parents.

(Anon.)

Foreword

In the last fifteen years or so, there have been many books published in the home–school field, describing and celebrating the increasing number of initiatives undertaken by teachers, parents and other professionals working in collaboration on behalf of children.

Yet a glance at the bookshelves confirms that the overwhelming majority of these have been written by professionals – educationalists in the main – writing primarily for a professional audience. Hardly any books within the home–school 'stable' have been written by parents themselves.

Eileen Gascoigne's book is therefore especially welcome, for she is a parent, writing from the perspective of a parent of children with special educational needs. Furthermore, in this book she has brought centre-stage the area of SEN, which has often, over the years, remained on the educational margins, and she leaves the reader in no doubt that she perceives SEN issues to be central within education. Her book will ensure that SEN becomes 'visible, accessible and accountable', to use her own words.

The publication of Eileen's book is timely, coming as it does at a time when schools have been setting their SEN policies, required now by law, and have begun to implement the Code of Practice, to which they must have 'due regard'. This means that schools are expected to take very seriously the principles of home–school partnership outlined in the Code of Practice, and they will have to demonstrate how they pursue such partnership ideals in practice.

Eileen Gascoigne's book will be a tremendous asset to parents, teachers and others in this task as her book closely follows the Code of Practice stages and discusses principles and action in detail. Other parents will feel encouraged to act upon her suggestions and heartened by her informed assurances, and professionals will gain from Eileen's incomparable parental insights.

Her message is challenging and inspiring to all.

Sheila Wolfendale
May 1995

Home and School – A Working Alliance

This Series, edited by *John Bastiani* and *Sheila Wolfendale*, brings together wide-ranging contributions which

* offer an assessment of what has been achieved
* explore a number of problematic issues and experiences
* illustrate developments that are beginning to take shape.

It will appeal to those with a special interest in and commitment to home–school work in all its actual and potential facets

Early titles will be:

Working with Parents as Partners in SEN
Eileen Gascoigne
1–85346–375–2

Home–School Work in Britain – review, reflection and development
Edited by John Bastiani and Sheila Wolfendale, with contributions from members of the National Home–School Development Group
1–85346–395–7

Subsequent titles will include:

Home–School Liaison and Minority Ethnic Parents and Families
Edited by John Bastiani

Working with Parents of SEN Children after the Code of Practice
Edited by Sheila Wolfendale

Parental Perspectives and Experience
Author to be announced

Parents and Children's Learning
Author to be announced

Introduction

The 1993 Education Act, and its Code of Practice on the Identification and Assessment of Special Educational Needs (SEN), incorporate and promote the concept of parental partnership to an extent previously unheard of in connection with SEN.

Parents have long been considered essential in many aspects of their children's education, and this includes a vast range of activities: helping their children learn and practise reading; providing them with the facilities to complete homework; attending parental consultations; going into school to help with cookery and other activities; participation in annual general meetings; involvement with PTAs; election of or participation as parent governors; helping at fêtes and bazaars; and so the list goes on.

Of course, not all parents participate in all or any of these. Indeed, in most schools, it is only a few active parents who can be seen at all the events, leaving the majority of parents outside the school's day-to-day activities. In many cases the participation of parents is additional to the activities of the school, rather than central to the development of the school's teaching and child management philosophy or policies.

When it comes to special needs, the participation of parents needs to be rather more profound. Encouraged into the partnership appropriately, most parents of children with special needs will be able to influence positively a whole host of educational and non-educational aspects of their child's development and schooling. According to the nature of their child's special needs, they can help the professionals understand the implications of their child's difficulties; they can advise on aspects of individual behaviour management; they can help to devise and implement joint home/school strategies; they can give guidance on physical management of the child in the classroom and wider school environments; and of course, they can also help with homework, reading practice and all the other things the 'active' parent gets involved with.

The demands on parents and professionals alike in establishing a meaningful, constructive, productive and sustainable partnership in special educational needs are many and challenging. The range of professionals who become involved, both generally in the SEN field and specifically in individual cases, adds a complexity of interdisciplinary co-ordination seldom encountered elsewhere in the practical implementation of an educational programme. The intensity of parents' feelings about the needs of their child, the possible routes to progress, the development to his or her maximum potential, and the danger of failure are all tangible. Emotions can run high, and professionals too can find themselves caught in bewildering exchanges where objectivity is lost and there is risk of the situation degenerating into heated argument.

Yet at the centre of this maelstrom stands a child, in whose interests these exchanges take place, for whose benefit both parents and professionals are working, and who will gain or lose according to the outcome. A way must be found to minimise the risk of conflict clouding the real issues, both at strategic level and in practice with individual cases; and where conflict does arise, the will and means must be found to minimise its destructive impact.

Not all issues relate to the minimisation of conflict, however. The lack of a framework within which professionals and parents can truly work in partnership results in lost opportunities for both sides to learn. Many parents would offer helpful insight into their child's difficulties, and suggestions as to how they might be tackled, if only they were asked in the right way. There are invisible barriers to parental participation. Even where teachers, psychologists and others believe they have opened doors, parents may feel intimidated, inferior and lacking in confidence to such an extent that they do not offer to add their own tremendous knowledge and experience to the equation. One of the very practical benefits of full parental partnership is that these barriers can be broken down.

Another benefit is wider access to professional expert input. If a child's needs do require investigation, and possible causes such as sensory, motor or linguistic impairments need to be evaluated or ruled out, the parents are the only ones who can access the specialist help, through referral to the various health agencies. Schools and LEAs are strictly limited as to the range of specialists from other agencies that they can call upon on behalf of a child.

Even without the need for external specialist advice, the parents' daily experience of their child is an important source of additional information that can help to complete the picture of a child experiencing problems. Comparison of the child's learning patterns in the home and school environments can often highlight the successful strategies to be developed, or can identify common stumbling blocks.

During any formalised assessment process, the 1993 Act's Code of Practice emphasises the importance of parental involvement in, and contribution to, the collective understanding of their child's needs. The information exchange has to be a two-way process: not only because parents need to participate in the decision-making about placement, but also because, for many children with special educational needs, out-of-school strategies as well as home–school co-operation all contribute to enabling a child to overcome his or her difficulties. These strategies in turn become an integral part of the child's specialised provision.

This book is designed to help education professionals realise where some of the barriers to parental involvement lie; to enable them to help parents to participate; to reduce the incidence or risk of conflict; and to achieve the underlying objective within SEN, which is to provide the most appropriate educational programme for each child so that he or she can achieve and succeed in his or her education.

So who do I mean by 'professionals'? For the purposes of this book, 'professional' is a wide-ranging term. It includes those readily recognised as professionals – paid employees with training and qualifications working in the field of education: class, subject and head teachers; special needs co-ordinators; learning support teachers; advisory teachers; educational psychologists; LEA officers.

However, I also extend the definition to include others working in schools, such as classroom assistants, welfare helpers and school governors; and beyond that, local councillors serving on education committees and special needs sub-committees. There are additional professionals in non-educational fields whose work impinges upon education in the SEN area, such as designated medical officers, speech and language therapists, occupational therapists, physiotherapists and social workers, as well as the decision-making management teams in both health and social services agencies.

There is an additional group that will gain increasing stature and importance over the coming years: the Named Persons. These are volunteers whose unpaid services are intended to facilitate positive parental involvement in the process of identification, assessment, provision and review of their child's special educational needs. Many of these Named Persons will be volunteers from within existing voluntary organisations, whose influence on educational policy and practice is increasing within the SEN field. For some professionals, this is a welcome involvement; for others it represents an intrusion. Although members of the voluntary sector cannot be considered as 'professionals' in the strict sense, I do believe they have a significant and positive role to play. Their understanding of the interplay between parent and professional will be essential to their role of facilitation.

The role of partnership in schools

Although this book is focused specifically on children at school with special educational needs, this does not confine discussion to the school context. Children from birth onwards will become school children at some stage; the accurate evaluation of their needs, at as early a stage as possible, is critical if the most appropriate allocation is to be made to meet their needs. The establishment of good working relationships between all professionals and the parents as well as among the professionals themselves during the pre-school phase can give both the child and the parent more confidence when making the transition to school. Conversely, difficulties encountered by parents with respect to professionals in the pre-school phase can have significantly deleterious effects on the confidence and trust that parents place in the professionals once daytime care and control is surrendered to the school.

The introduction of the Code of Practice and its full implementation in schools as well as LEAs during 1995 means that, for the first time, the regulatory framework requires *all* teachers to become involved not only in the identification and assessment of a child's special educational needs, but also in the constructive involvement of parents in the processes. All schools will have in place SEN policies detailing their own approach to identification and assessment, and how they anticipate working with parents. All governing bodies must now cover special educational needs specifically in their annual report to parents; all governing bodies must designate one governor to oversee the SEN activities of the school. In other words, SEN becomes visible, accessible and accountable.

What the Code of Practice sought to achieve was the universal implementation of what was seen to be good practice in those schools already actively committed to special educational needs. I do not underestimate the burden this places on individuals within our schools. The requirement to implement the Code of Practice comes at a time when the slight easing of the national curriculum as a result of the Dearing review is more than counterbalanced by the budgetary stringency imposed on both schools and LEAs by recessionary forces at a national level. Different individuals face different consequences according to their roles; everyone faces tremendous challenges.

The SENCO (special educational needs co-ordinator) is the individual who bears the brunt of the additional administration and organisation within the school. In some schools the SENCO will occupy a dedicated full-time post within the learning support department, be qualified and experienced in SEN, and already have in place the myriad contacts and networking that will be required to carry out their duties.

In many schools, however, and particularly in primary schools, the SENCO will be a teacher who has taken on the role as an additional duty, for a variety of reasons; these reasons range from a wish to apply some specialised knowledge, training or expertise to a desire just to help the less able children. Those who volunteered to be the special needs contact point before the 1993 Education Act may now be seriously reappraising their prior enthusiasm and questioning their ability to cope.

The SENCO is the linchpin of the school's SEN policy: advising in its development, and responsible along with the head teacher and the designated governor for its implementation; applying its principles in individual cases; being the in-house resource for all other members of staff to call upon; named in public as the parents' key contact point in respect of their own child's special educational needs; and the filter through which the school's contact with external specialists and other agencies will take place. All this is often in addition to full-time or part-time classroom and curriculum duties.

Many SENCOs will not have had any specific SEN qualification or training; INSET (In-Service Training) and training funded by GEST (Grants for Education, Service and Training), to introduce the Code of Practice and LEA procedures, will not cover all the SENCO's needs, and is unlikely to be consistently applied or equally accessible within any one area or LEA. There is certainly no national standard of training or support for SENCOs.

The variation in type and severity of special needs that can be encountered in the school setting is vast. In addition to clear 'diagnoses' that arrive with some children in the reception class, there are innumerable special needs that will require identification and assessment during a child's school life. Indeed, even for those whose diagnoses are declared on school entry, the extent and impact of the condition still need to be evaluated once the child is exposed to school routine and demands. Further, continued monitoring is required to identify any new needs that emerge over time.

How many teachers are confident that they will be able to identify and assess a child's possible SEN? Of course, all teachers are able to identify when a child is failing to keep up with the class; continuous assessment of a child's progress is part and parcel of the teaching job. But how many class teachers, form tutors or subject teachers are able to differentiate between the various possible causative factors in a child's apparent lack of progress? Hearing impairment, visual impairment, specific learning difficulties, expressive or receptive language difficulties, emotional difficulties or dysfunctions, fine and gross motor skills – all these are just some of the possible causes of a child's inability to progress alongside his or her peers. The difficulty is that teachers are not trained to conduct such differential diagnoses. Further, unless and until a child's difficulties become severe enough to warrant a Stage Three or Stage Four intervention, no outside specialist help is likely to be called upon to assist in the evaluation. Even where this external advice is sought, often the teaching staff will need to work through and with the parents to identify the most appropriate referrals.

The role of partnership beyond school

Educational psychologists represent a major resource for both schools and parents alike. With training and expertise in many different types of learning difficulty, they provide invaluable information, insight and advice on the assessment of a child's difficulties, as well as possible strategies for overcoming them. Even here, the partnership with parents is paramount. An educational psychologist, no matter how experienced or well-trained, is likely to see an individual child for a few hours at the most, in a limited range of settings. Again, only the parents can offer the insight into the general abilities or difficulties of their child, in all settings and under all circumstances. The parents' contribution to an educational psychologist's assessment is, I believe, vital, as is their full understanding of the outcome of the assessment. For the child still has his or her difficulties outside the classroom setting, and consistency of understanding and approach to help him or her at school and at home is essential if real progress is to be made.

For LEA officers involved in statutory assessments, the partnership with parents should be of twofold value. Firstly, in individual cases, the benefit of a meaningful parental contribution to the assessment is enormous. Secondly, in the general development of the SEN service, the contribution to be made by parents can be immeasurable. Often LEAs develop procedures and systems to cope with or to facilitate parental involvement, without actually listening to the views of parents on how they would like to be involved. The recent introduction of GEST funding to LEAs for developing parent partnership schemes is a recognition at least at national level that partnership extends beyond individual case work.

Partnership issues for other 'professionals'

School governors are now responsible for ensuring the proper development and implementation of SEN policies in their schools. These policies are expected to say a great deal about how the school works with parents in the field of SEN; it follows that governors too must ensure that they facilitate parental involvement in the development of policy as well as in its implementation and monitoring. This involvement in policy development must include parents of children with special needs in the school, not simply the parent governors already in post, even if they themselves have direct experience of special needs. The parent governor's experience of working with and in the school is by definition different from that of the 'ordinary' parent.

LEA councillors are ultimately the ones responsible for developing the political and economic environment within which SEN services are developed, especially those relating to central support services. It is essential that parental views are expressed at this policy-making level. In this way, all levels of SEN policy development – school, LEA procedures, and LEA education policy – carry forward the vision of partnership embodied in the Code of Practice.

Many professionals are concerned that opening their doors to parents in this way, particularly at more strategic levels, will expose them to increased conflict. After all, for many years, their only experience of parental involvement may have been through complaints, at appeals, or in judicial reviews, or referrals to the Ombudsman. On these occasions, the more vociferous parent is very likely to appear in a confrontational, aggressive and implacable mood. This is frequently because other channels of communication have been effectively blocked by professionals who – understandably – have been afraid to expose themselves to risk.

Where parent partnership schemes have been introduced, they have grown into co-operative and mutually beneficial forums for discussion and debate, and offer an opportunity for all parties to enlighten each other as to their concerns, constraints and opportunities for constructive development.

Named Persons

The concept of the Named Person, introduced in the final version of the Code of Practice, is one that is still open to debate. Even within the voluntary sector, keen to develop the idea of informing and empowering parents, the Named Person has become something of a two-edged sword. However, the idea remains constructive, even if the details require some additional thought.

For parents whose children are undergoing assessment for their special educational needs, there is a bewildering array of formal procedures, parades of experts and specialists, and a great deal of uncertainty. Parents do need help from a sympathetic but well-informed source. I believe the Named Person fulfils that role. Once on board, the Named Person is 'attached' to the parent concerned for the post-statement implementation and review stages, procedures which for many parents can be as traumatic and contentious as the assessment process itself.

Named Persons will begin to appear at parent/teacher meetings and annual reviews. It is an extension of the partnership debate to examine how this additional relationship can be managed.

Many Named Persons will themselves be parents of children with special educational needs. Many are motivated to become involved in helping other parents because they have skills of counselling and arbitration to offer. Some will get involved as a result of their own negative experiences, hoping to help other parents to avoid some of the same pitfalls. Just a few may even be using their position as a Named Person to continue playing out their own anger with the system.

Named Persons are required once a new Statement is finalised. (A 'Statement' in the context of this book is the document issued by an education authority taking responsibility for SEN provision for a named child.) Over time, Named Persons will become involved throughout the assessment process itself; and still further on they will become common in cases of children whose Statements were already in place when the 1993 Education Act came into effect, as they come due for review or reassessment.

Partnership between disciplines

Although this aspect is not central to this book, it does impinge upon parental partnership, as the parents are often the only people to have met with every professional involved with their child, be they from education, welfare or medical agencies. Parents are often bewildered and angered by the apparent lack of co-operation between professionals from different disciplines, when they themselves have trusted each one with the care of their own child. This topic is picked up in Chapter 3.

This book is not a definitive guide to the law on special educational needs. Other authors are better qualified to provide that guidance.

The purpose of this book is to explore the opportunities for professionals to encourage and exploit the participation of parents in the full process: from identification of a child's difficulties, through both school-based and statutory assessment, in devising programmes to address the child's difficulties, to monitoring and reviewing progress. It does not seek to be prescriptive, as I recognise that the circumstances surrounding each child, class, school and LEA will differ. I aim to provide avenues to explore and options to consider.

The objective is to explain the parental perspective: to put into context the parents' viewpoint on their child's education; to explore the broader psychological, emotional and practical environment within which parents operate. All this helps to ensure that a meaningful partnership can develop.

The book is intended to be read not only as a single exposition, but also as a practical guide to help professionals get the best out of their partnership with parents, to be referred to as teachers and others approach different aspects of special needs in different cases.

The first two chapters examine the parent as a person: what has happened to them, to their expectations, hopes and fears for their child; what feelings they have had to come to terms with; the experiences they have undergone in dealing with professionals over time; the impact on them and their wider family of having a special needs child. These chapters are intended to build a picture of the new partner who will join the professionals in their task of helping the child to succeed.

Chapter 3 examines the concept of partnership and seeks to establish the broad framework within which the working relationship is designed to develop.

Chapters 4 to 9 follow the structure of the Code of Practice, and highlight some of the practical implications of partnership through the various stages of identification, assessment, provision and review, as well as in the development of school SEN policies.

Finally, Chapter 10 examines the matter of complaints and appeals – events which effective parent partnership should be able to reduce if not in frequency, then at least in vehemence.

Throughout the book, case histories have been used to illustrate various points, either to highlight the difficulties encountered and to offer suggestions of how they have been or could be overcome, or to highlight good practice. These examples are taken from real case histories. Names of the children and parents have been changed, and schools, LEAs and other agencies are not identifiable. This is to enable the reader to concentrate on the principles contained within the case history, rather than to point the finger of blame at any particular individual or organisation for past errors.

Appendix A is a summary of a survey among parents undertaken during the spring term 1995. Appendix B is a reproduction of the guidance notes produced by ASpEN (Action for Special Educational Needs), a parent support group, to help parents write about their child's special educational needs. Appendix C includes a brief directory of some of the organisations that can help parents and professionals with various aspects of SEN.

I am the mother of three children, all of whom have special educational needs. In terms of the Code of Practice stages that need to be gone through to obtain SEN help, at the time of writing they are respectively at Stage Five, Stage Four and Stage Two (going on Three). The eldest, sixteen in 1995, has had a Statement since he was four. He has attended in turn a mainstream nursery, a special school, a special unit attached to a mainstream primary, a mainstream primary, a mainstream secondary, and currently residential special school.

The middle son, thirteen in 1995, is now being assessed under Stage Four, having been supported in mainstream primary and secondary schools with varying degrees of success.

The youngest was diagnosed as having specific learning difficulties, and at the age of nine was transferred to a school that specialises in dyslexia, where he has begun overcoming his difficulties. He does not have a Statement.

The direct experience of seeing these three children through the processes is used throughout this book to highlight certain aspects of the professional/parent relationship; experiences with these three also appear as anonymised case histories. However, my experience is not limited to these three. I am a founder member of, and volunteer worker for, a parent support group called ASpEN. ASpEN (Action for Special Educational Needs) is a registered charity, offering direct support to parents in Bedfordshire, Buckinghamshire and Hertfordshire, with wider telephone and postal support nationally.

ASpEN offers support to parents of children with SEN, irrespective of the nature or severity of the child's difficulties. The volunteers in ASpEN have effectively been operating as 'Named Persons' since 1992, and are actively involved in using their experiences to support the training of new volunteers taking on the role of Named Person under the Code of Practice. ASpEN's philosophy of preventing conflict and promoting mutual understanding, rather than encouraging an adversarial stance, is reflected in this book. Part of ASpEN's work includes close liaison with LEAs and other professionals, and I myself have been involved not only in policy discussions, but also in training sessions for professionals to help them understand the parental perspective. I sit on the SEN policy panel of a local education authority as parent representative, and represent ASpEN on the Parent Advisory Group set up by that LEA to elicit parental views on service development and operation.

As a result of my involvement in ASpEN, I have been involved in hundreds of cases, offering information and insight for parents and professionals alike to facilitate understanding among all parties, in order to resolve satisfactorily issues both for individual children and at policy and service development levels.

I am indebted to the many officers, teachers, psychologists, councillors and others who have enhanced my own understanding of the professionals' viewpoint, as well as the many parents who have offered their own experiences specifically for inclusion in this book.

Most of all I offer my appreciation to my family for their support to me while writing this book.

1 Parental experience

The diagnosis of a special need in a young child is a very distressing event for parents whenever it happens, whether at birth, in the early months, or when the child is already at school. Recent research by SCOPE (previously the Spastics Society) has examined the experiences of a number of parents whose children were diagnosed very early in their young lives. Readers are encouraged to study a copy for full details of this research, which demonstrates the response by parents to professionals according to the factual content, timing and attitudinal approach of the disclosure.

There are important conclusions for educational professionals in this research report. First of all, the fact that a child has been diagnosed as having a certain condition or syndrome many years earlier does not mean that the emotions experienced by parents have faded away by the time their child begins school. Although most parents do accept their child's disability or handicap, it would be wrong for any professional to assume that the parents have therefore 'come to terms' with it. It does not take very much for the emotional reaction to diagnosis and disclosure to come back to the surface in later months or even years. Many of those included in the SCOPE research were parents of adult people with handicaps of one sort or another. Their memories of the moment – or phase – of disclosure are still very real and very detailed. This applies not only to the facts surrounding the event – what the doctor was wearing, who was in the room, what the trees outside the window looked like, the actual words used and so on – but also to the emotions experienced at the time. Parents don't only remember how they felt, they experience all over again those same emotions and reactions: despair and anger; rejection and love simultaneously for their child; bitterness at the attitude of professionals – or conversely, respect for the professionals who dealt positively with them.

When a parent comes to a teacher in school, or to a psychologist at an assessment, or to a gathering of professionals in a case meeting, these feelings are still there, kept in check for the most part, but rarely far away. Often they come back to the surface in a most unexpected way, and at a most inopportune time. Even when the events that initially caused the strong feelings are in the distant past, those feelings can very easily be resurrected without warning.

I can remember being in a case meeting going through my son's history. The occasion was the introduction of a new professional to the ever-extending network who had been involved over the previous eleven years. One would have expected that, after eleven years of covering his history with various professionals, time and frequency of retelling would have inured me to the full emotional reaction. Part way through recounting the history, I was bewildered as to why this professional, and my husband, were looking at me with increasing concern on their faces, and could not understand why the words in my head were failing to come out through my mouth. Eventually, my husband leaned over, took my hand and said, 'Stop trying to talk.' Only then did I realise that I was crying, the tears rolling down my cheeks, my eyes getting redder and redder, and my voice cracking. It took me almost twenty minutes to recover sufficiently to rejoin the conversation, which my husband had been able to pick up in the meantime.

(Mrs K, talking about her son N who has Asperger syndrome.)

Professionals who come into the picture long after the child's needs have first been recognised, or an initial diagnosis made, must remain aware of this. Just because a parent has been coping with their child's disability or handicap for the past three to five years does not mean that they are objective about it. They can review their child's needs quite calmly, offer suggestions as to how the child can be accommodated and handled in the classroom, and listen to suggestions made by professionals regarding home–school links. Do not imagine that this calm exterior reflects a calm inner self. When a child first ventures into school, away from the constant care and supervision of their parents, there is an additional cause of fear and anxiety that by handing over a significant portion of their child's welfare to another person or organisation, they may be failing to maintain an appropriate level of support.

The transfer of any child from the parent's complete care into the hands of professionals whose job it is to look after up to thirty individual children is very difficult for any parent. Surrendering that responsibility for the special needs child is particularly so. Over the pre-school period, the child's parents will have learned to adjust their whole way of life to accommodate the special needs of their child. In addition to possible physical adjustments to their home, there will have been a change of normal parental priorities; the needs of that child will have been paramount, even at the expense of the needs of other children in the family. Perhaps the parents may not have been able to go out, finding baby-sitters almost impossible to come by; it may affect the way food is prepared, or what foods are allowed; it could affect the way mealtimes are conducted, or the bedtime routines; account might need to be taken of the specialist toileting needs, how far the child can walk; special equipment might need to be carried everywhere. The list is endless. Every family makes its own myriad tiny and major adjustments, to cater for the all-day, all-night, everyday needs of their child. The overriding concern is that this intensity of care will not be possible in the school setting; parents fear that their child will suffer as a result.

The range of emotions and reactions that parents go through once they realise their child has problems is vast. Parents come to the analysis by starting from their role as a parent. It sounds obvious, but unless this is borne in mind, all the rest does not follow. When a professional deals with a special needs child, no matter how empathetic, kindly or caring that professional is, a certain detachment and objectivity underlie every interaction and observation. But parents feel responsible for their children, so whatever happens to the child is taken very personally by the parent. The parent bears the responsibility; the parent takes the blame. This propensity to shoulder blame leads to the most damaging emotion of all – guilt.

Guilt is one of the most fundamental and persistent reactions that parents – particularly mothers – experience. Once the habit of guilt has formed, it is a very difficult one to break. Everything becomes 'their fault'; a real persecution complex can develop very easily. The slightest criticism or negative observation is taken as a personal criticism, for which blame must be acknowledged.

> Fact: N had not bonded. Cause: it was my inadequacy as a mother – he didn't fail to bond with me, *I* had not bonded with *him*.
> Fact: N had not started talking. Cause: it must be my fault for not talking to him enough, not reading out loud to him enough.
> Fact: N did not relate well to others. Cause: it must be because I had not mixed enough with mother and toddler groups, coffee mornings, playgroups.
> Fact: N could not cope with change. Cause: clearly I had been too wedded to routine; or too prone to impulsive changes of routine.
> Fact: N had fixated behaviour. Cause: well, that *must* be my fault for not providing a diversity of stimulation for him in his early months and years.
>
> (Mrs K, regarding her son N, who has Asperger syndrome.)

When a parent meets a teacher, taking this child into the nursery or reception class, or even later on in the child's schooling, the guilt can be resurrected all too easily. Table 1.1 illustrates just how readily the wrong interpretation can be placed on quite innocent comments by a parent prone to guilt and self-blame.

14

Table 1.1

Comment	Interpretation
'He doesn't do his homework.'	'I am not helping him enough with his homework.'
'She won't ask for help.'	'I've brought her up to be too independent.'
'He doesn't seem to know how to play with the other children.'	'I should have taken him to more playgroups.'
'She has not developed pre-reading skills.'	'I should have spent more time reading with her.'
'He's very keen on Postman Pat, isn't he?'	'I let him watch too much television.'

Professionals should ask themselves just how these parents might misinterpret what they say. Not all parents will do so, but as the risk is quite high, particularly for parents whose children's difficulties manifest themselves in bizarre, odd or inappropriate behaviour, it is important for teachers, psychologists and other professionals to consider re-wording what they say, or leading into their observations in a more circumspect way.

After guilt come bitterness and resentment: the inevitable 'Why me?' It's not that the parents wish it on someone else, but rather an angry response to the grief they are going through. As a result of this bitterness, parents often become perceived as having a huge chip on their shoulder. Subsequently this can get in the way of meaningful discussions with the seemingly endless procession of professionals they have to deal with, who are totally objective about their child and his/her difficulties, and seem unable to comprehend why the parents appear to have such an 'attitude problem'.

Denial can play a big role in the way parents react to their child's disability. Even where the disability, learning difficulty or handicap is quite obvious, many parents still indulge in some form of denial. This is frequently experienced in the first few weeks and months after diagnosis or realisation. 'There must be some mistake', 'They've got the medical records mixed up', 'He'll grow out of it', or 'It'll go away if we ignore it.' Denial is often identified by professionals in both medical and educational fields, and is not confined to any particular type of special need. In many ways it can be seen in a negative light; the parent who remains in denial will never 'come to terms' with their child's difficulties, and so will not be able to help the child progress.

On the other hand, there is also a positive benefit to denial. The parent who refuses to accept all the predicted limitations on their child is more likely to work very hard to help him or her overcome the difficulties. Stories abound of children for whom a consultant's prognosis was very poor, but whose parents proudly display their child's achievements. It is the fighting spirit that springs from a refusal to accept the poor prognosis that motivates many parents to work hard with their child to help them achieve their full potential. It is also this very fighting spirit, and fundamental belief in their child, that causes many parents to come into conflict with the education authorities and professionals. It is the parents' belief that their child *can* do something, with enough support and encouragement, that is in conflict with the professional's acceptance of the poor prognosis.

> They said she'd never recover at all. She'd be unable to walk, control her body, see, talk. But look at her now. She is trying to stand: holding on to furniture. She can make about seven different sounds for different things. She was actually watching the television last night – got really upset when I changed the channel.
>
> (Mrs J-T, whose daughter V suffered severe brain damage during an operation at the age of seven.)

In this sense, then, parents rarely 'come to terms' with their child's difficulties; the question is, should they? 'Coming to terms' with it means to give in: to accept that this is the best they can expect; to believe that they should give up hope of progress. Too many parents have proved the professionals wrong in the past; too many parents are willing to try anything to maximise their child's potential to achieve and succeed. It is anathema for them to 'come to terms' with the limitations presented to them.

Hope is a very positive emotion, most of the time. Hope is what keeps people going when all the evidence is against them – in any sphere of life. Hope is what keeps rescue teams searching the rubble for survivors after an earthquake; hope is what motivates doctors to keep trying to resuscitate a heart attack victim; hope is what keeps researchers looking for a cure for cancer. Hope is what keeps parents trying and fighting for the best possible provision for their child.

However, even hope can have its downside. Hope keeps many parents looking for a 'cure' for their child's difficulties. It means parents coming to professionals time after time with yet another research article about a new teaching method, piece of equipment or device that will transform their child's life. Some of these may be blind alleys; but many do turn out to be beneficial, and when a parent meets rebuttal and disbelief from the professionals, the rift between the two parties becomes wider.

Anger is an ever-present threat. Parents are angry with themselves for failing to provide a 'normal' life for their child; they are angry with the professionals and agencies they meet for failing to help them access all the appropriate support and provision for their child. It is often an unreasonable anger, directed at the people who really cannot change things, but just happen to be there. Thus school secretaries and clerks in education authorities take verbal abuse from parents when their head teachers or managers are not available to come to the phone, or school staff are threatened when an appointment is not forthcoming with the educational psychologist. The anger is born of the bitterness and frustration of the situation parents find themselves in. No one likes to feel helpless; and when parents are made to feel helpless to resolve their children's difficulties, the anger can be overwhelming.

Many psychologists now accept that a parent of a handicapped child needs to grieve, just as if a loved one had died; but the day-to-day reality of coping with the child means that this grieving process is severely curtailed. They are supposed to be brave; they are supposed to love this child they did not ask for, forget the one they expected and hoped for. They are not allowed to resent their child, only resent the situation. Yet it is natural. When we expect a baby, we expect a normal baby, one whom Granny can bounce proudly on her knee, one who will play with toys in the toddler group, one who will make friends at school, who will progress through nursery, primary and secondary schools, hopefully to university, college, or at least to a useful occupation. Someone who sadly will grow up to be independent, leave home and start their own family. Mums buy the books and magazines that talk about pregnancy, labour and the new-born baby in glowing terms of normality. The shock is immeasurable once the parents realise that none of this applies any more, that to get information about how to look after *their* baby they must ask in whispers at the library enquiries section, or send off to some distant and remote charity for a booklist.

There is a need both to grieve for the child they did not have, and to come to love and accept the child they do have. These parents can and do love their special needs children; they just need time sometimes to turn that love into a practical, positive attitude.

All these emotions – and more – are experienced by parents throughout their child's life, and not just at the point of diagnosis. It doesn't only happen when the child's disability is profound and diagnosed early. In addition to being aware of the emotional baggage parents bring with them to the school situation after years of coping with their special needs child, teachers, psychologists and others working in the education system need to be prepared to encounter these feelings when a child is identified as having some special educational needs after starting school.

Most of the children assessed at Stage Four are assessed after they have started school. All of the children on Stages One to Three will by definition already be at school. That means that many of the parents whose children have special needs will first hear the fact from a teacher, special needs co-ordinator or psychologist. These professionals may not come up with the diagnosis, but they may be the first to say to a parent, 'We have some concern …'. No matter if the parents had already had that concern themselves, or even if they had initially expressed their worries to the teacher, it still remains a shock for them to hear a professional say it, or to confirm their fears. As parents they may suspect, and hope it is not true; once a professional confirms there is a need to be concerned, any pretence is over.

It does not have to be a serious special need to trigger these feelings and reactions. A slight delay in learning to write, a suggestion of a few extra sessions out of the classroom with another teacher 'who knows how to help children catch up', will be enough to start the negative spiral of denial, blame-throwing and anger.

One of the most provocative situations for parents is when the first hint that a child has any difficulties at all is a deterioration in the child's behaviour. When collecting her child at the end of what she believes to be a normal school day, a mother is not prepared for the teacher calling her over 'for a quick word'. When that quick word becomes a litany of misdemeanours, then Mum's defences are down, and an emotional reaction almost inevitably ensues.

> It got to the point where I wouldn't go into the playground to collect V, because I knew his teacher would call me over to tell me what he'd done today. I got fed up with the constant negative. No one was suggesting solutions; I felt I was being blamed. OK, I know he is a bit difficult at times. But if I have difficulty at home with him, I sort it out. I don't expect to be called in for every little misdemeanour in the classroom: they should sort that out. And they never told me anything good, what he had achieved or succeeded at, only what he'd done that was bad. You can only take so much negative all the time.

(Mrs J, whose son V had become disruptive in class.)

The use of diagnostic labels

Labels, or diagnoses, are very useful things. Once a name is given to a condition or set of symptoms, it can provide a focus for further investigation, both by parents and by professionals. For example, Down's syndrome children often suffer hearing difficulties, heart defects, or visual impairments, among other things: so for the medical staff, the initial diagnosis of Down's syndrome can provide a further checklist for them to identify – or eliminate – associated difficulties. For parents, a diagnostic label can often give them access to a voluntary organisation which can provide not only further information, but also a source of emotional, psychological and practical support both from helplines and from meeting other parents. Just knowing what heading to look under in the library or encyclopaedia is a tremendous first step on the road to discovery, and often to accepting the fact of their child's disabilities.

For many parents, this road of discovery can become very involved; their pursuit of information knows no bounds, and extends to examining clinical and psychological research papers, attending conferences intended for a specialist audience, and corresponding with leaders of world opinion, in the search for useful advice on how to help their child. This pursuit of knowledge can become an end in itself, and such parents will become very knowledgeable about their child's particular area of difficulty.

These parents should not be condemned for their zeal. Many parents feel that teachers and others are critical of their intensity of knowledge and interest in what the professionals believe to be their own domain. Parents with such advanced levels of knowledge can often intimidate professionals, such as teachers and psychologists, and this can lead to a confrontational experience. What parents are trying to do on such occasions is say, 'Look, I know a lot about this, because I've taken the trouble to find out; as a professional, you should also know this much if you are to help my child.' Many 'experts' quite understandably resent this apparent criticism of their own levels of knowledge, but most parents are only trying to add to the general understanding of their own child, to support his or her progress. A few are trying to 'score points', but these are really a small minority of parents, whose own need for recognition as an 'expert' on their child is paramount. They may have felt inferior to professionals in the past, and want to show that they are worthy of inclusion in the critical discussions about their child's future. A positive attitude to real partnership will help to overcome and may even prevent this type of confrontation.

There is an endless list of labels and descriptors for the different types of special need that any teacher, psychologist or LEA officer may encounter. Some are useful as a broad description: some are helpful indicators of the type and severity of the special educational needs. Very few, if any, are actual definitions of educational – or even non-educational – needs. Some are well recognised definitive medical terms, such as autism, Down's syndrome, spina bifida and cerebral palsy; some diagnostic labels have patchy acceptance among professionals, with lively debate still raging in research circles, and these include dyslexia, dyspraxia and attention deficit disorder; others often appear to be interchangeable terms for the same broad group of symptoms, such as dyslexia/specific learning difficulties, and autism/pervasive developmental delay. Some are specialist medical diagnoses for which there is as yet no overall interdisciplinary agreement on how to treat or on prognosis, such as semantic–pragmatic disorder and Asperger syndrome. Others are no more than categories of provision that have come to encompass a generality of learning difficulties: among these would come moderate learning difficulties, severe learning difficulties and emotional and behavioural difficulties.

Parents and professionals alike need to be wary of the overuse of and over-reliance on such diagnostic labels. One of the dangers of labels is that they can often obscure a full assessment and evaluation of a child's needs. Clinging on to one label as the definitive one can prevent parents and professionals alike from identifying associated or concomitant difficulties in a child with special needs. There are many common overlaps and 'joint appearances' that can be overlooked if too much reliance is placed on the first label to be applied.

For example, language disorders often appear together with dyslexia or specific learning difficulties. There is some thinking that they may be connected, that the cause of each lies in damage to the same area of the brain. However, they do not always occur together. 'Pure dyslexia' or 'pure language disorder' can exist as diagnoses in their own right. By using one label primarily, there may be a tendency not to look for the other difficulties, putting all the child's needs down to aspects of the one condition. In consequence, appropriate strategies and provisions to help the child overcome their difficulties may fail to be identified.

X is a case in point. At the age of three, he was diagnosed as having dyspraxia, on the basis of his poor muscle tone and poor gross and fine motor control. Only when he reached seven, when the dyspraxia-oriented provision began to fail, did his mother begin to consider that his expressive and receptive language difficulties might be problems in their own right. He also showed signs of dyslexia. The initial label, while quite valid, had obscured everyone's ability to identify each of his individual needs.

Some diagnoses can be made earlier than others: for example, dyspraxia is increasingly being identified in children of pre-school age. Higher-level language disorders are not usually apparent until the child is five or more, while symptoms of dyslexia can be identified when the child begins to work on pre-reading and pre-number work. Down's syndrome can be identified within days or weeks of birth, while autism may not be identifiable until a child fails to develop normal social interaction or communication, often between two and five, depending on the type and severity of the condition in a particular child.

If a child has more than one type of difficulty – not as uncommon as many people may think – then sometimes the first diagnosis can overwhelm any subsequent attempts to identify additional or associated specific difficulties. There is a danger sometimes that all a child's difficulties can be put down to the primary diagnosis: a child with autism may have all social interaction difficulties put down to poor communication skills, when in fact they may also be hearing-impaired.

A child having apparent difficulties across the curriculum may be 'labelled' as having moderate learning difficulties, when in fact a moderate receptive language difficulty may be preventing his or her understanding of what is required, reducing consequent performance. Children with this type of difficulty will also fare badly on normative testing, so may be routed through MLD provision, without any attention being paid to their specific language needs.

Children of apparent average ability who begin to disrupt the class may start to be labelled as 'EBD', when in fact they may be of above average intelligence, with some undiagnosed special educational needs holding them back to average performance. Their frustration level becomes higher, and their only response is to behave in an unacceptable or inappropriate manner. Their behaviour difficulties are easy to identify; they are assumed to be of average ability, so they are routed into an EBD stereotype, rather than fully assessed to identify their full range of needs.

Another risk with diagnostic labels is that they can often mean different things to different people; they certainly mean different things in respect of different children. If one teacher uses the word 'dyslexia' to another, do they really mean the same group of specific learning difficulties? Is there an accepted definition of the word 'dyspraxia'? Is Asperger syndrome a type of autism or a separate syndrome altogether? Just what is semantic–pragmatic disorder? At what level of performance do we set moderate and severe learning difficulties? Many of these questions remain quite academic; whole conferences are held among interested professionals to debate definitions and argue the finer points of interpretation. Little wonder then that misunderstandings occur between professionals and parents. This does not mean that everyone has to avoid using the terms, rather that any inbuilt assumptions must be recognised when each term is used, and that individuals should check with each other that everyone is making the same assumptions.

So labels are useful to an extent, but when the time comes to determine the most appropriate provision to meet the child's individual needs, there is a clear requirement to 'unbundle' the diagnosis and identify very specific items for action. This can, unfortunately, be one of the key causes of conflict between parents and professionals during the assessment and provision process, as parents seek to cling on to a label that they are comfortable with, and find it difficult to accept other interpretations of their child's history.

For many children there are no labels. They present with a collection of symptoms, none of which forms a medical condition in itself, and which taken together do not constitute a known syndrome. Parents of these children often long for a 'label', for two reasons: firstly so that they know where to start looking for information, to find out more, and possibly to find a peer group of other parents they can talk to; and secondly so that they can use a simple phrase to explain to others what is wrong with their child. For these parents, it is often more difficult for them to understand what they can expect for their child, for there is no body of evidence or collection of case histories to give them a clue; they feel they are fighting in the dark.

Day-to-day life with a special needs child

It must be recognised by professionals that having a special needs child in the family affects all the members of that family. It affects all the relationships within the family, and the family's relationships with the rest of the community. It is a daily experience, not just an event at diagnosis or assessment. Any child brings joys and worries; but when a child has special needs, the joys may be less frequent, to be found in small things, while the worries are constant and often all-encompassing.

For children with severe difficulties, daily life is a constant struggle of special routines, as the whole family's way of life often has to revolve around the needs of the handicapped child. Making up feeds, changing incontinence pads, spoon feeding, lifting and carrying – these are all daily and hourly realities for many parents, year upon year. The additional stress of a formal assessment can often prove overwhelming.

> I know about my daughter's needs; I have to tube-feed her every day, change her catheter, carry her upstairs, lift her in and out of her frame, wheelchair and so on. But I could scream when I read it in black and white. It somehow seems to be so final, so impersonal.
>
> (Mr J-T, father of V.)

For some parents, the stress becomes too much for the marriage to bear; having a special needs child can cause its own friction between mother and father, for a whole variety of reasons. Perhaps one parent has a different approach to the child's odd behaviour, wanting to be more strict and disciplinarian, and believes the other parent's more 'understanding' approach is counter-productive. Perhaps one parent is thought to spend too much time looking after the special needs child and not enough with the rest of the family. There may be a dispute over whether or not to take advantage of respite care or short-term fostering. One parent may be feeling guilty at not being able to come to terms with their child's handicap as readily as their partner appears able to do. They may just be very tired. Marriages often break down after the arrival of a child with special needs, even if those special needs are not diagnosed early on.

> It is very hard from an emotional point of view to take on the system – you are dealing with people who view you as a case number. Many times my phone calls were angry and rude as I could not get any sense out of those involved. I wrote numerous letters to the LEA; I badgered people and generally made sure they didn't forget I was around and would not let the subject drop.
>
> I really fought for my daughter – it took over my whole life for a time – my family suffered, my relationship with my husband suffered – the whole experience was destructive.
>
> There are no words which adequately convey what it is like to live with a child with special needs – you are treated differently by friends and family – the very professionals who are there to help and support seem to do the very opposite – they should never tell angry parents that they 'know how they feel' – they do not!
>
> I am beginning to write my daughter's story for her and my son to read when they get older so that they may understand better what a permanent and dramatic effect her language disorder has had on all of us – she will always have problems but she is the most loved, wanted child in the world.

(Mrs P, whose five-year-old daughter has a language disorder.)

It is becoming recognised that siblings of a child with special needs often experience difficulties themselves; they are often late to mature socially, may go through periods of anxiety and stress, and can display within the classroom special needs of their own which they keep hidden at home. Some special needs are familial, and a brother or sister may have a milder version of the condition; some may result from learned or copied behaviour strategies, for example when an older brother or sister is autistic or has other communication, social or behavioural difficulties.

When the parents are undergoing periods of stress, the other children in the family are undoubtedly affected, and their performance at school, or behaviour both at school and at home, may deteriorate. Teachers of a child whose brother or sister has significant special needs should be sensitive to these pressures and stresses, and be alert to their possible consequences. This does not mean that the other children's difficulties should be merely ignored or 'allowed for', but that they should be recognised as special needs in themselves; it may be worth identifying such children on the SEN register, after consultation with the parents, so that strategies can be agreed beforehand for handling any difficulties as they appear. What is equally important is that any difficulties seen in the brother or sister are not merely explained away by the fact of the handicapped sibling; the other children in the family may have special educational needs in their own right.

Brothers and sisters are often embarrassed by their sibling's difficulties, and their own friends can often gibe at them: 'Your brother's thick', or 'Your sister's a goon', simple childish banter that can cut a child to the quick. They may react by protecting their brother or sister, and risk isolating themselves from their own peer group; they may react by agreeing with their friends, and then feel resentful about their brother or sister, or guilty for taking sides against them.

It can often be very difficult for grandparents to come to terms with the fact that their grandchild has special needs. Many grandparents grew up in an age when anyone with a handicap was 'put away'; they are unused to dealing with the idea of a handicapped person at all, let alone within their own family. In this case, they may have put pressure on the parents to have the child adopted; in some cases, they may refuse to acknowledge that the handicapped child exists at all.

My mother still writes, and phones, and we still visit. But I cannot take G. When G was born, mother said 'get rid of it', and has never referred to her since. When mother rings up and asks after the family, she asks after each of the other children, but pointedly misses out G. G never gets a birthday or Christmas card from granny, like the others do.

(Mrs O, mother of G who has Down's syndrome.)

My mother-in-law was fine until we first said we thought something was wrong with Q. When we said we thought he might be autistic, all communication broke down. That was ten years ago. I haven't spoken since, and she refuses to acknowledge that I or our children exist. She still talks to her son, my husband, occasionally.

(Mrs L, mother of Q who has mixed difficulties including language delay, dyslexia and dyspraxia.)

However, some grandparents can be very supportive, and take an even more active role in supporting the parents than they would otherwise do. This can be a particular boon where baby-sitting is difficult to arrange through the usual channels. Conversely, it may cause feelings of resentment in the parents that they are still reliant on their own parents, reducing their own self-esteem as they cannot cope.

Relationships outside the family are also often strained by having a child with special needs, and different parents devise different strategies to cope with this.

We have two sets of friends. One set whose children are also handicapped in some way. And another set who have nothing to do with disability. The two are kept separate. We don't share our daughter's disability with the second group and we don't try to have a normal life with the first. It's the only way I can cope.

(Mrs A, whose daughter I has Down's syndrome.)

It can affect how parents relate to the community around them, in particular the parents of other children at their child's school. Many children are very accepting of a friend in class who is 'a bit different', and often enjoy helping them understand what is expected, or with particular tasks. The attitudes of other parents, however, can be very isolating. This is particularly so if the child's difficulties include odd, bizarre or difficult behaviour. Parents encourage their children to 'play with that nice little girl' rather than the difficult one. The other parents regard the parent of the special needs child with some suspicion, and can effectively exclude them from the socialising in the playground, or at school events. The child with special educational needs may find it difficult to make friends; many young mums find their own friends among the parents of their children's friends, but this route to an established peer group may be denied to the parents of children with special needs. If the child attends a special school or special nursery, contact with their peer group may be further diminished, as the special school may not be very local, and the child may go to and from school in a taxi or school bus.

Even teachers have been known to compound the problem of child and parent peer group relationships, by indicating which children may be suitable playmates for each other, either indirectly or overtly.

Our daughter's relationship with a friend (a girl) at Class 1 was stopped by the class teacher who influenced that child's mother. So our daughter's friendship was stopped. Our relationship with the teacher was damaged and our friendship with this child's parents is today nothing. Our daughter was extremely wounded and hurt and has come to accept but yet to realise and can't understand what did she do wrong to deserve this.

(Mr L, whose daughter R has general learning difficulties.)

Practical points

- *When first diagnosing:* Be honest but sensitive. Give time for the parents to take in what is said. Be aware of the emotional reactions that may result from initial disclosure or diagnosis.
- *When meeting with parents informally:* Consider what you are trying to communicate, and be sensitive to how the message might be received.

- *When meeting with parents during formal assessments*: Be aware that parents may experience a full range of emotions, from anger and rage to hope and optimism, just through re-examining known facts about their child.
- *When dealing with siblings of a special needs child:* Be aware that they too live with the pressures and stresses of their brother or sister's difficulties. Be alert for similar or other difficulties arising in siblings.

2 Parents as partners

In order to determine how professionals can work in partnership with parents, it is important to examine what 'parents' are: how they might approach partnership; why they behave in certain ways; how these behaviours can sometimes block a working partnership; how they can often facilitate a good working relationship; and how all professional partners can work with them to elicit the most productive involvement.

Parents are not a homogeneous group. They come in all shapes, sizes, attitudes and emotions. Chapter 1 looked at some experiences of parents outside the education system: their responses and reactions to the fact that their child is not 'normal'; their day-to-day stresses and pressures that can colour their dealings with all the professionals with whom they come into contact. This chapter looks at how these factors affect the way parents enter the processes of identification and assessment, and therefore how they are equipped or handicapped in their bid for full partnership. The aim is to help professionals understand the way parents enter discussions – their state of mind, their motivations – so that from the first encounter onwards, the partnership is productive and constructive, and not derailed by misconceptions and emotional overlays.

Types of parent

There are distinct groupings of parents, who have common behaviour patterns when they deal with professionals. How they appear and behave does not necessarily correspond with how they are feeling inside. If professionals only respond to them according to how they appear, the risks of partnership breaking down are high.

The articulate, assertive, educated parents

How do they appear? These parents, without the complication of their child's special educational needs, would probably be the one any teacher would prefer to deal with at parents' consultation evenings. They are confident when speaking with professionals, appear to understand what professionals are talking about, and approach any discussion about their child with equanimity and assertiveness. They may not always agree with the professionals involved, but disagreements tend to be unemotional, and differences of opinion can usually be reconciled in a civilised way.

When their child has special educational needs, these are the parents who can find their way around the system; they will already know, or readily find out, their rights; they will exercise those rights; they will seek external, independent advice; and they will accept their own place around the meeting table as equals with the professionals involved. Being well educated, they have no fear about disagreeing with any of the experts they encounter. Many of them will have identified an area for research, possibly spurred on by a formal diagnosis of some sort, and will have gained a tremendous amount of knowledge specific to their own child's areas of difficulty.

What are they really like, inside? The outward appearance of calmness, self-confidence and assertiveness can often mask these parents' true feelings. Like all parents of children with special needs, these parents are subject to guilt, feelings of inadequacy and helplessness, and can be as bewildered by the educational system and SEN procedures as any other. Often their determination to maintain a calm and 'professional' demeanour prevents them from acknowledging openly when they are unsure of something. This can lead to many false assumptions being made by the professionals whom they meet. There may be an underlying assumption here that the parent can cope with bad news about their child's progress. The fact that they appear able to cope within the professional arena, and that they do not act in a confrontational manner or react emotionally, may cause professionals to treat these parents with more openness or directness than they can really cope with. Diagnoses or assessment results may be presented starkly, as if to another professional, when what they really need is a more diplomatic and sensitive presentation of the facts. They do not want to be misled or told half-truths, but they are still emotionally attached to the child in question, and need recognition of this by professionals.

> I felt so silly. Here I was, running a helpline for other parents to call for support and advice, being told my son was not coping in school and might need a formal assessment and Statement. I'd been through it all over the years with my older son, but it didn't prevent the shock reaction. I kept calm during the meeting, even shared a joke with the teachers about the Statementing system. I couldn't get out of the school fast enough. I cried all the way home, hid in the bathroom to recover, and then carried on crying for about three days. I felt awful. I thought I should have coped, but at the end of the day I was just as vulnerable as any other parent at the same stage. I don't think the professionals ever realised.
>
> (Mrs K, regarding her son, E.)

There is often an assumption that these parents understand the SEN processes and procedures, particularly in formal assessment and Statement reviews, so professionals may not spend enough time explaining things. A further assumption is that this type of parent fully understands their child's difficulties, so professionals such as psychologists or teachers often skip that part of their explanation when discussing teaching programmes or specialised provision. They may also assume that the parents fully understand the educational programmes that are referred to in documents or discussions; while this may be the case for some parents, many will merely smile kindly and feign understanding, not wanting to appear ignorant.

As these parents present themselves in a professional manner, the professionals they meet may be more likely to expose weaknesses in their own organisation or agency, or in the system as a whole. On the positive side this may enable the proactive parent to develop their own strategies to overcome inherent difficulties in the system. Conversely it can reduce their faith in the ability of the professionals to make adequate and appropriate provision for their child.

The angry, knowledgeable parent

How do they appear? These are the parents who come to their dealings with professionals well informed, yet unable to approach the discussion in the calm, quiet manner of the first group. They are more likely to harangue the professionals they meet, viewing them with some contempt because their own 'expert' knowledge exceeds that of the 'experts' they meet. They may be dismissive of any perceived attempt to divert the conversation away from their own agenda, and angry if their own knowledge is in any way questioned or disagreed with. They often start their conversations with a challenge, and may be rigorous in their ability to quote chapter and verse of various Acts of Parliament, Statutory Regulations, Department for Education circulars and noted legal precedents.

What are they really like, inside? While feeling on an equal footing with many of the more highly specialised professionals involved in their child's history and management, many of these parents have low regard for the more generalist professionals they encounter; they may perceive their own knowledge as greater than that of the teachers, psychologists, LEA officers and so on. They are angry that the 'experts' with whom they have to deal seem to care so little about their child that they have not even bothered to find out more about their child's type of difficulties. They are less likely to accept that the professionals have constraints of time and resources preventing them from reading around a subject, or from undertaking further training. Neither do they accept that there might be professional disagreement about the subject of their child's disability or learning difficulty: or, if such disagreement exists, that their own 'experts' should not be preferred. These parents may often be inept at handling professional meetings, partly owing to lack of experience, but also because they are emotionally tied to the subject under discussion – their child.

It is difficult, when faced with an aggressive or confrontational parent, for the professionals to remain calm. However, these parents, just like the first group, are concerned only with their child's welfare. They care about their child's education, and have a belief that, with appropriate provision, their child can overcome or work around their disability or learning difficulty. Their sole aim is to ensure that that appropriate provision is made available.

The acquiescent or submissive parent

How do they appear? These parents will agree to almost anything any professional suggests. They generally do not proactively pursue independent research or advice from other specialists, and will trust almost totally in the judgement of their child's teachers, GP, paediatrician or educational psychologist. In many ways, they are an easy group for professionals to work with. They readily answer any questions put to them by professionals, but rarely offer information spontaneously.

What are they really like, inside? These parents do not have confidence in their own status as 'expert in their own child', unless reminded of their true knowledge and experience. They may be tentatively waiting for the professionals to give them guidance and direction; they may prefer to 'leave it all to the experts'. While they may hope that one of the professionals will give them an opening to offer more information, or ask further questions, they may be unsure of how to break into the conversations to do so proactively. The fact that they do not express their own opinions readily does not mean that they do not have them. They may feel that they have not been asked for their views, and subsequently resent this.

A further complication within this group of parents is their unwillingness to criticise openly any of the professionals involved with their child. They fear that this would have detrimental consequences; for example they may believe that if they say they are not happy with a certain aspect of the school's dealing with their child, the school might then be less supportive of them and their child in the future. They may appear content, because they do not complain; they are as likely as any other type of parent to be dissatisfied. The result is that their dissatisfactions often build up inside, and it may be many years later, perhaps when their child is due to move on to the next phase of school, or out of school altogether, that the accumulated frustration and criticism burst out.⌉

The 'uncaring' parent

How do they appear? Not all parents place, or appear to place, education at the top of their agenda for their child. For many adults, their own educational experience may have been less than satisfactory. The average educational attainment for adults in this country is far less than that for the average teacher, and certainly less than that achieved by many of the other professionals; these may have two or more degrees as well as further vocational qualifications. Some parents appear to be unconcerned that their child is falling behind, unable to do maths, or becoming disruptive in class. Their attitude comes across as ⌈'That's your problem: you're his teacher, you cope with it.'⌉They may appear to have low expectations of their child within the school setting, or in life generally⌋. They may appear to have given up trying to help their child overcome a disability or learning difficulty. They may not appear to be helping their child at home with the continuation of programmes devised in school for behaviour management, or literacy skills development, or with homework. Some may appear to have domestic problems, which may be assumed by professionals to be a causative factor in their children's difficulties. The poor parental attitude is seen to be passed on to the child, who subsequently fails to thrive educationally.

What are they really like, inside? Many parents are simply afraid of the educational system. If they have had a poor educational experience themselves, they may have low or no expectations of the system for their child. In their own general priorities for life, qualifications or academic skills may come very low down, below getting a job, becoming independent, or just surviving. For them, 'getting a job' may have little or nothing to do with 'getting an education'. Educated middle-class people regard these two as synonymous, as do most professionals working in education. This attitude may be offensive to parents for whom 'education' is an irrelevance.

For some parents in this group, however, there may be other factors. Their understanding of their child's needs may place 'education' much further down the list of priorities than educational professionals might wish.

> We don't want Q to start full-time schooling when he is five. We want to concentrate on physiotherapy, because we believe that the daily physio he is having now will enable him to maximise his physical potential, leading to maximum access of his educational opportunities later. He is socially rather immature, so the argument about 'peer group' does not apply. The physio will

have less impact on him after the age of about seven, so then we will be happy to accept full-time schooling.

(Mrs V, about her son Q, who has cerebral palsy.)

There are still other parents whose experience of the educational system in respect of their special needs child has made them bitter about the system, and hold the aims of educational professionals in less high regard than might otherwise have been the case. This may be particularly so for a child with emotional and behavioural difficulties, or an undiagnosed learning difficulty, where any trust or faith in the professionals has dissipated over a period of time.

The angry, ill-informed parent

How do they appear? A little like the angry, knowledgeable parent, these parents are likely to behave in a confrontational manner. Appeals to reason may not have any effect, and may eventually lead to more angry exchanges. Often these parents will resort to writing in order to express their dissatisfaction with the way they are being dealt with, or harangue professionals and their clerical or secretarial staff on the phone, often rather abusively.

They are among the most difficult to deal with, and probably the group that most professionals would prefer to avoid if possible. Interaction with these parents may be brief and succinct, and often revert to formalised, even legalistic responses from the professionals, probably out of self-defence. It is easy to get angry with such parents.

What are they really like, inside? At the risk of repetition, these parents care deeply and desperately about their child. They may misunderstand the nature of their child's difficulties; they may have latched on to a particular label, and have read a little about it, yet they may not be able to identify accurately their child's specific needs. They may have difficulty accepting one type of special need – for example, slow learning – yet be willing to accept that their child has another type of difficulty – for example, dyslexia.

How the professionals explain the particular difficulties in their child will be as important as what difficulties are identified. These parents are very likely to be confused about the way the educational and SEN systems work, and often misunderstand the varied, separate roles of different professionals. Having explained everything to the psychologist, they are then angry when another professional asks about the same thing. They may not understand the relationship between psychologist and class teacher, or medical officer and therapist. They are bewildered by the complexity of the inter-professional network, and indignant that bureaucracy appears to get in the way of their own child's welfare. In some cases, they believe such obstructionism is deliberate, with professionals seeking to limit the resources they make available.

The fighting parent

How do they appear? Some parents appear to take more interest in 'the fight' than in their own child's needs. Once they have engaged with professionals or education authorities, they seem to take delight in pursuing their argument, while losing sight of the underlying objective – that is, to access the most appropriate provision to meet their child's needs. Like the angry, knowledgeable parent, they are likely to be able to quote in detail Acts, Regulations, Circulars and court proceedings, and will readily seek recourse to legal advisers. They may seek to make general points about the way the system operates rather than focus only on their own child's case.

What are they really like, inside? While their child's interests are their main concern, they perceive the professionals they meet as the 'gatekeepers' to the system. Battling with the gatekeeper therefore becomes paramount. Efforts to work in partnership, while difficult, will pay dividends once these parents perceive that everyone is pursuing the same objective. They are readily frustrated by a system that purports to be there precisely to help their child, yet appears to throw up obstacles at every turn. Time delays and administrative errors are particularly annoying for these parents, for whom the 'answer' seems obvious, and who cannot understand why the professionals can't see it.

For many of these parents, they are actually not far wrong. The system is supposed to exist precisely to help children like theirs. Often the parents and professionals at the front line agree on the child's needs and the provision required to meet them. However, the procedures are also there to assess whether any other, as yet unidentified, needs may exist, or to clarify the severity or nature of the difficulties, and to evaluate the options for provision. This aspect of the process is less transparent, and is a possible cause of these parents' dissatisfaction.

The special needs parent

How do they appear? In many ways, all parents of children with special needs are themselves special needs parents. The emotional and psychological baggage most parents carry with them can handicap them in approaching the whole process. There is a specific group, however, whose needs must be kept in mind when professionals begin to deal with them. Parents may suffer from the same type of difficulties as their children; many learning difficulties have an inherited element. Dyslexia, speech and language difficulties, communication disorders, general learning difficulties and emotional difficulties can all be found in parents as well as their children. Some parents may find it difficult to express their views and convey their knowledge in writing, and many parents find it difficult to do so orally in front of professionals. They say what they mean, in the only way they know how, yet often fail to express it in a way that is 'acceptable' or comprehensible to the professionals. When they review the reports of their contribution, or summaries in a Statement, they are angry that their views appear not to have been taken into account. Sometimes what they have said is understood differently by the professionals listening to them.

What are they really like, inside? They have an opinion about their child, but feel frustrated in not being able to find the right words to express it in a way that the professionals either understand or take seriously. It is easy for these parents to feel patronised by professionals who smile sweetly and nod wisely, but in the end apparently take no notice. They feel marginalised; their views and knowledge seem to be trivialised.

Parents with learning difficulties are very likely to be confused by the things they hear or see written down, either about their child or about the process. They will need more time for explanation, and may need explanations many times over.

These subgroups of the species 'parent' are not meant to be an exhaustive list. Some parents may move from one category to another during the period of their child's schooling. Some parents overlap between groups. Others are unique, fitting no stereotype at all. What is important is that how parents appear, and what they are really like, are not necessarily the same thing. For professionals working with parents in special educational needs, it is important to recognise the person within, rather than deal only with the parent as he or she appears.

Parent vs. professional

So, how does a parent measure up as a partner?

The following list outlines how parents see the differences between themselves and the professionals they deal with in the identification and assessment of their child's needs. (For a summary, see Table 2.1 on p.38).

- *Paid/unpaid.* This is one of the most significant and easily identified differences between parents and professionals, and can be one of the major causes of resentment among parents. Not only do the professionals get paid, but they get paid whether or not they do their job well or efficiently. When parents perceive an error has been made, or some communication has not got through, or a file has gone missing, they experience a level of resentment towards the professionals involved that is almost directly related to their perceived salaries.

- *Compulsory/voluntary.* With very few exceptions, perhaps where a child with known special needs is adopted, parents have not volunteered to have a child with special needs. It has happened to them, without warning and without their consent. No one ever gave them the choice of having a baby with special needs or not; no one asked them which type of special needs they felt they could cope with.

  The professionals working in the field of special educational needs are, to a large extent, doing so voluntarily. They have chosen this career path, elected to work in education, therapy or special needs, and therefore also have the right to choose not to be involved. Professionals, to the parents' minds, enjoy the work they do, and gain fulfilment from their involvement in special needs. Even teachers who joined the profession for the mainstream experience must have accepted that they will at some stage need to deal with the special needs children as well as the high achievers.

  Many parents, while loving their children and enjoying many aspects of their growth and development, do not 'enjoy' the fact that their child has special needs. Very few find 'fulfilment' in the additional challenges their children's special needs provide. *Post hoc* rationalisation leads some parents to say how much more enriched their lives have become as the result of having their special needs child, but most, if being really honest, would rather have had an entirely 'normal' family.

- *Permanent/part of career development.* From the moment their child is born, whether or not the diagnosis is made then, parents become the parents of a special needs child. This role lasts until their special needs child becomes an adult; then they can look forward to a 'promotion', to being the parent of a special needs adult. As parents, they are the only ones to have a truly long-term perspective on their child's development. They are the only members of the 'partnership' who will be there throughout every assessment, every annual or termly review, every phase change, every life stage. When the stress and strain all gets too much, the parent has to hang on in there, because that is what a parent is and does. A parent cannot delegate except on an occasional basis, perhaps to respite carers or caring relatives. Once the responsibility is taken on, it sticks.

For the professionals, their involvement in any one child's case is temporary and often episodic. The child's teacher may only have that particular class for one academic year, and in any event that child is only one in a larger class. The psychologist will see the child for a few hours a year at most. The other specialists may see the child for a few hours a week, if giving ongoing therapy, or for half an hour a year, at a check-up. When the next review comes along, it is likely that the officer, or psychologist, or advisory teacher, or class teacher will be different.

If the going gets too tough for the professionals they can apply for another job, seek promotion, or leave altogether. This option is generally not open to parents.

- *Continuous/sporadic.* A parent's responsibility for their special needs child is continuous; it lasts for twenty-four hours a day, seven days a week. With the possible exception of respite care, or if a child is staying in a residential special school, there are no breaks. For many parents whose child has a severe disability or complex mix of needs, even day school can be seen as a respite. However, if the child presents a particular behavioural difficulty at school, or is taken ill, the parents are likely to have to intervene even during the school day.

All professionals work given hours, even if in addition to the contracted time they take reports home with them, or take on extra duties, or extend their working day to fit in all their workload. The very nature of a professional working contract is that there are weekends, evenings, bank holidays and leave entitlements available for the professional to recoup. Parents do not have this luxury. If they are waiting for an answer to a particular question about their child's difficulties, they can't just put them in a filing tray and wait for the next report! If the parents are feeling tired or ill, they cannot take a 'day off'.

- *Untrained/trained.* When a parent finds out that their child has special needs of whatever sort, they are left to find out for themselves how to deal with the difficulties they might encounter. They learn as they go along, find out from books or parent support groups, snatch tips and guidance from some of the professionals they encounter along the way. They are largely self-taught, and have found out how to help their child often through trial and error. Theirs is 'hands-on' training.

All the professionals involved in special educational needs have taken some specialist qualification to start them in their chosen career. They have access to further training, through either INSET or additional courses made available through the LEA or other authorities. While undergoing training they have opportunities to work alongside experienced professionals.

- *Inexperienced/experienced.* This comparator is something of a two-edged sword. On the one hand, it is accepted by most parents that the professionals they meet are experienced in their field, even if not in the specialism of their own child's particular difficulties. They accept that they as parents do not necessarily know or understand what other children of a similar age or disability might be achieving, how they are behaving, or what they are struggling to do.

  However, the context of the 1993 Education Act and its Code of Practice, and indeed the basis of all legislation, regulation and service development since the Warnock report, place a different construction on the term 'experience'. The whole process of identification, assessment, provision and review is based on an individual child's needs, not the generality of needs within an overall category or group. Within this context, the most experienced partner in the process is the parent.

  The parent is most experienced in their own child. Any professional involved may be able to compare, either through normative testing or from experience, how that child measures up against any other children of a particular age, type or category of special need, but will not necessarily know that individual child very well at all. Professionals use their experience to categorise and generalise; parents use their experience to focus on the individual needs of their very individual child. The nature, depth and breadth of their experience are specific to the case in hand, and therefore have a validity in their own right.

- *Isolated/networked.* Most professionals will have opportunities to share their concerns, ideas and experiences with an appropriate peer group. When they are under stress, there are associates and colleagues, as well as organised support agencies such as professional associations or trade unions, to offer help on both a personal and professional level. If a teacher, psychologist or LEA officer reads a report on a child that contains technical information they do not understand, they have a network of able and available specialists within their organisational structure or associated agencies to whom they can turn for advice, interpretation or information.

  Parents cannot do this. Some parents are members of voluntary organisations or support groups, which can provide varying levels of support. These are often run by volunteers who may not be readily available, and may not have had any specific training. Many parents – perhaps most parents whose children are at Stages One to Three – will not have such a group readily available to them. If no specific diagnosis or 'label' has been assigned, there may be no group to call. They will perhaps have friends to turn to, but these may not understand about the stresses they are undergoing as a result either of their child's needs, or of the assessment process.

Many parents are actually reluctant to join voluntary organisations or support groups, for a variety of reasons: they do not want to be constantly reminded of their problems; they are afraid of getting too deeply involved in their child's disability; meeting parents of adults with the same special needs as their own child may depress them and reduce their hope for the future.

Parents of children with special needs are isolated in a more general sense. They begin to lose all common ground with their own peer group. Friends with whom they grew up, and who began their families at the same time, start to drift away. Their parenting and family experience become fundamentally different, so that any common ground on which the initial friendship was based becomes less and less.

- *Subjective/objective.* Of course parents are subjective, passionate, emotional about their child's future. It would be unreasonable to expect anything else. Often this creates a dilemma for parents in dealing with the professionals they meet. Each professional can remain objective when reviewing a child's special needs; they may be touched, they may care deeply, they may have empathy, but they are not emotionally involved or attached. The parents often remain suspicious of the advice professionals provide because of this. They know that the professionals make practical judgements that might not be based solely on their child's needs. Financial and other resource issues come into the equation. 'The efficient use of resources' can be a damning phrase to a parent's ear when they want only the best for their child.

  The educational professionals are only obliged to provide what is appropriate; health professionals are only obliged to provide what is available; parents seek what is best. Parents are often afraid that any emotional response from them will invalidate their participation.

  > Once they have broken down in one meeting, many parents give up the fight: they are not prepared to make a fool of themselves again; they are not prepared to go through the agony.

  > (I K, a worker with a parent support group in London.)

- *Whole child/one aspect.* Many parents become bewildered by the specific educational focus that teachers, educational psychologists and LEAs bring to the assessment process. Much of this is a result of the pressure of law and regulation; the educational system and procedures for identification and assessment of special educational needs make this inevitable. The parents see their child in a more holistic way, rarely separating educational, therapy, social and health aspects. Although the Code of Practice requires specific action on the part of other agencies to support the assessment process, there are yet to be developed coherent national or local policies or strategies that will enable professionals from the different disciplines to work closely together for any individual child. The requirements in the Code only apply to identification and assessment; there is yet to be an agreement on how provision is to be co-ordinated between agencies. For example, when a pre-school child has speech therapy, specific clinic-based therapy is often withdrawn once the child starts school, on the understanding that any further provision will be made under the Statement. The availability of occupational therapy and physiotherapy for children who need them is not consistent either between authorities or between schools within an authority.

It is important that these differences are recognised and accepted in the development of partnership between professionals and parents. They do not provide reasons for avoiding the partnership, but provide a foundation on which meaningful partnership can be developed.

Practical points

- Accept parents for what they are: people who know their children well.
- Accept parents' expertise, even if it appears to question your own.
- Be willing to listen, not just to what is said, but to what is meant.
- Offer parents partnership.

Table 2.1 Differences between parents and professionals

Parent	Professional
Unpaid	Paid
Compulsory	Voluntary
Permanent	Part of a career developmenment
Continuous	Evenings off, weekends off, holiday entitlement, Christmas and bank holidays off
Untrained	Trained
Inexperienced	Experienced
Isolated	Network of colleagues
Passionate/emotional/subjective	Objective
Whole child	Focused on one aspect

3 Partnership – a conceptual framework

There is an assumption that everyone knows what 'partnership' means, that everyone has the same understanding of the word. This, like many assumptions, is at best misleading, and at worst quite dangerous. While most people will know instinctively what they mean by 'partnership' in the course of normal conversation, its specific and particular use in the context of special educational needs and 'parental partnership' must be defined before any debate can proceed about its implementation, otherwise it risks becoming just another piece of jargon that serves only to obfuscate rather than clarify.

Foreword:16[1]

Although the Code of Practice features parental partnership very strongly, nowhere is it defined; clearly, there is an assumption that we all know and agree on its meaning. Paragraph 16 of the Foreword to the Code states:

> [The fundamental principles of the Code] include the principle of partnership. If effective provision is to be made for children with special educational needs, it is essential that schools, LEAs, the health services, social services, voluntary organisations and other agencies work very closely with each other, and that all work closely with parents.

The booklet produced by the Department for Education, *Special Educational Needs – A Guide for Parents*, takes the idea a step further:

> Your knowledge, views and experiences as a parent are vital in helping your child to develop. Your child is likely to make most progress if you, your child's school and the LEA all work together in partnership.

and

> You, as a parent, have a right to take part in decisions about your child's education and to be kept in touch at all stages. Your views and support are very important.

Sadly, for many parents this is not the reality they encounter when their child begins to experience difficulties at school, or when they approach the assessment process. For many parents, their invitation to be involved in their own child's education consists of being asked for a rerun of their

---

[1] Numbers in small boxes refer to the relevant sections of the Code of Practice.

child's developmental history, and being informed about what the professionals or various agencies have decided they will provide.

⌈The first thing about partnership in special educational needs is that it is a complex, multiple partnership.⌉The description in the Foreword to the Code of Practice fails to recognise this. It talks about professionals and agencies working together, then jointly working with the parents. Too often, this leads to the assumption that partnership with parents is a one-to-one link. The underlying presumption is that 'professionals' can be formed into a single, homogeneous group, and therefore only one link needs to be established between them and the parents.

The difficulty with this approach is that it assumes a pre-existing collaborative arrangement on the part of the professionals, and that communication within the professional partnership is readily achievable, leaving only the individual parent in any specific case to be added to the equation. Yet everyone knows, in practice, that the professional players vary according to each case and within a case over time. This inappropriate concept of parental links, this expectation of a single link between the 'professionals' on the one hand, and the parent on the other, leads to the question: 'Which one of the professionals is best placed to forge links with the parent?' It is by trying to answer this that the fallacy of the initial proposition is uncovered. Consider the following options (and see Table 3.2 on p.54 for a summary).

- *The class teacher* (assuming the child is already at school; or it may be the early years advisory teacher in the case of a pre-school child). The class or advisory teacher clearly already knows the child concerned. He or she may even have been instrumental in identifying the child's difficulties. The teacher will also know, or at least have met, the parents. If Stages One to Three have been invoked, then it is likely (although unfortunately not necessarily the case) that the teacher will have discussed the child's needs with the parents, and some agreement will already have been reached over how the child's needs are to be addressed.

  There are drawbacks, however, to this individual being the link between parents and professionals. Should the child need the additional input of a range of specialists outside the school, it is likely that the class teacher would be unable to forge links with these other professionals, and would therefore fail to be the professionals' representative in the partnership. An advisory teacher specialising in the early years may have appropriate links with psychologists and some health professionals, but these may not be formalised or generally applicable to all cases.

  Additionally, class teachers are unlikely to be very familiar with the procedures required at Stages Four and Five, and therefore not in a position to offer useful guidance to parents at these stages. If the child requires alternative placement, again the class teacher is not in a position to advise the parents on what alternative provision might be available.

In addition, the class teacher in a primary school is likely to be involved with any particular child for only one or two years, and the advisory teacher for early years generally moves out of the frame once the child has started school, leading to loss of continuity.

It is important also to remember that, in some cases, parents find themselves in conflict with the child's teachers, believing – often erroneously – that their child is not learning because of poor teaching methods or standards. It is not a pleasant conflict, but if positive strategies for partnership are to be established, it must be recognised that these situations occur.

- *The head teacher.* Many of the same arguments apply as to the class or form teacher. The additional benefit is that the head teacher is likely to be a constant over more years than a class or form tutor; however, this is outweighed by the fact that he or she is less likely to have detailed knowledge of the child, and may have been involved only in somewhat more formalised discussions with the parents. Most head teachers in mainstream schools will have experience of only a few formal assessments or Statements, and their experience may not be generally applicable to any one particular case.

- *The SENCO (special educational needs co-ordinator).* This individual offers perhaps the best option for a school-based link between parents and professionals. However, his or her involvement in Stage One is likely to have been minimal, and so detailed knowledge of the child cannot be taken for granted.

  Furthermore, the SENCO is as hampered as other members of staff within any particular school, in that they will not have access to information about other types of provision, except in a relatively superficial sense. For parents who may need to consider special school placements and in particular residential placements, the SENCO may only be able to provide patchy information which could be misleading. There is also some concern that SENCOs will not have ready access to all the other professionals who may be involved with a child, such as medical specialists or social services personnel.

- *The educational psychologist.* While the educational psychologist may be in a better position to provide information about the process and the system, their involvement with the individual child only begins at Stage Three. Many parents will need to be involved with a range of professionals during Stages One and Two; clearly the psychologist will not be able to assist there.

Once the educational psychologist is involved, the issue becomes one not only of how well the psychologist can represent the 'professional' side of the equation, but also how accessible they are to parents. Many parents are anxious about 'bothering' the psychologist, and the generally stretched nature of the psychology service in most areas of the country means that they do not have the time available to act as the link between parents and professionals. Educational psychologists may not have direct access to other professionals involved, particularly those within the medical specialisms.

- *The Named Officer* (LEA officer who co-ordinates a statutory assessment). At Stage Four this individual is the link person for all other contributors to the assessment process. It would seem obvious that, at least during the statutory assessment process, the officer takes on the responsibility of link between professionals and parents.

  However, in most cases, the officer will not have met the parents. In reality, officers generally only meet parents when there is a significant problem during the assessment, such as a fundamental disagreement by the parents with information or advice contained in the draft statement or its appendices. Furthermore, the officer is very unlikely to know the child; he or she will know of the child, but even this is incomplete until after all the advice has been gathered and evaluated. Asking the officer to be the link person for all aspects of the partnership would place unreasonable demands on the time and resources of these professionals.

- *Social worker.* Where a social worker is already involved with a family, for example through the provision of respite care, this can often be the best option. The family is likely to trust the social worker, and a strong working relationship has generally been built up over time. For the vast majority of parents, however, there is no social worker involvement. For a few families, such involvement may be for rather more negative reasons, such as care orders or other support for families in crisis.

  Social services departments do not necessarily have formal links in place with other agencies as a routine, but only on a case-by-case basis, or at broad policy level. This again severely limits the ability of a social worker, even when involved, to take on the full responsibility of parent/professional link person. They also may not know in detail how the SEN process works, and although they can offer support, are probably unable to offer the full range of advice and information required.

- *Medical officer, therapist or other specialist.* By definition, these individuals stand to one side of the SEN system. They provide advice, but are not pivotal, and so are unlikely to be able to provide a filter

Table 3.1

Partner	Stage(s)	Partner links
Named Officer	4, 5	Head teacher Educational psychologist Medical officer Social worker Parents
Head teacher	3, 4, 5	Class teacher SENCO Educational psychologist Named Officer Parents
Form/class teacher	1, 2, 3, 5	Parents Head teacher SENCO (Therapists if ongoing therapy provided in school)
SENCO	2, 3, 5	Parents Head teacher Form/class teacher Named Officer
Educational psychologist	3, 4, 5	Parents SENCO Form/class teacher Named Officer (Head teacher)
Medical officer	4, 5	Parents Specialist therapists Named Officer (Head teacher)
Therapists	1, 2, 3, 4, 5	Parents Medical officer (Class teacher if therapy provided in school)
Social worker	1, 2, 3, 4, 5	Parents Named Officer
Named Person	4, 5	Parents (Named Officer – depending on local Named Person scheme)
Independent specialists	3, 4, 5	Parents Medical officer (stage 4)
Parents	1, 2, 3, 4, 5	Named Officer Head teacher Class/form teacher SENCO Educational psychologist Medical officer Therapists Social worker Named Person Independent specialists

Figure 3.1

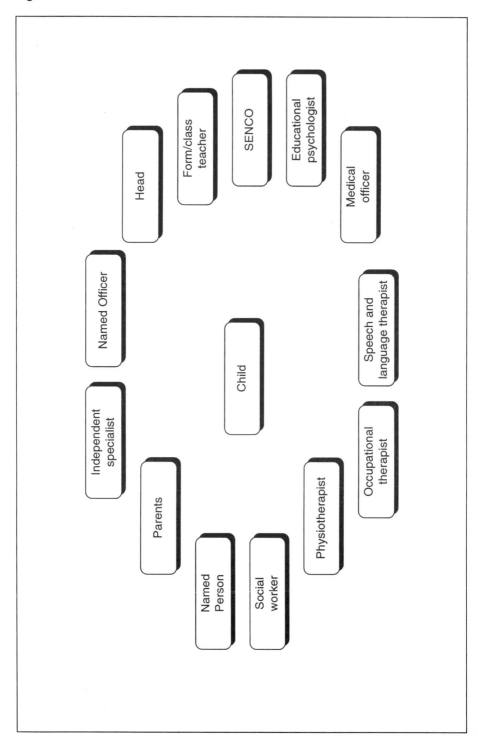

through which information can flow between parents and professionals.

So, if it is so difficult to provide links between professionals on the one hand and parents on the other, what hope is there for the concept of partnership?

The fault lies not in the role each professional plays, but in the assumption that professionals form one group, and parents another, requiring just one link between. In reality, the partnership is a multiple one. It is further compounded by the fact that, in every case, the individual partners are different people, and the matrix changes not only for each child but for any individual child over time. The number of potential – and real – combinations is almost infinite.

The survey reported in Appendix A shows that children may see ten or more different medical specialists during investigations into developmental or learning difficulties, in addition to the teachers, educational psychologist and SENCO. For most children, the figure lies somewhere between three and seven. The permutations become endless, and no specific framework or set of guidelines will ever be able to accommodate all the different possibilities.

Table 3.1 shows the stages at which each might become involved, and with which other partners they are likely to have ongoing contact.

It is clear from this that it is only the parents who are definitely going to meet or communicate with each of the other partners. No other individual will be involved at each interface. From this it becomes logical to suppose that the parent is best placed to act as the critical link between all partners. The parents offer the best option for ensuring that all partners stay fully informed and appropriately involved. Further, the parent is the only constant partner in the process over time, throughout all stages.

The difficulty is that many parents are not well equipped to do this. This means either that the whole idea of partnership becomes unworkable, or that effort has to be put in to facilitate the parents' full involvement.

What is important is the principle of partnership. Figure 3.1 shows a graphic representation of some of the possible 'partners' in any individual case.

From this, it can be seen that the parents form just one section in the overall partnership ring, with the child as the central focus for everybody. Each partner has a different perspective on the child, and contributes their own understanding of the child's needs.

In any partnership, it must be accepted that different individuals, different partners, will bring to the group different skills, perspectives, knowledge and experiences. The whole concept of a multidisciplinary approach to assessment and provision must acknowledge this. What has to be added, however, is the acknowledgement that parents have an equally valuable set of skills, perspectives, knowledge and experience that not only add something to the process but are irreplaceable.

Chapter 2 demonstrated that parents have a unique view of their child's difficulties and long-term prospects. They can offer much more than a regurgitated developmental history. If they are only ever asked for information about the age at which their child first walked, talked or rode a bicycle, the qualitative elements of their perspective will be lost. When the parents are involved in an appropriate way, the extra dimension can fundamentally change everyone's view of the child and his or her potential for achievement.

> W is a little girl with athetoid cerebral palsy. When the draft Statement was issued, her mother looked at all the professionals' reports and found she could not disagree with their content. They were accurate reflections of the assessments that had been carried out. W could not control her muscles to make 'purposeful' movements; W could not speak; W was almost totally blind, being able only to distinguish light from dark. W was destined for provision that could care for her and make the most of her tactile skills and sensitive hearing. But something was missing. When her mother was encouraged to speak about W, a different picture emerged. 'Last week, I put W on her mattress in the lounge and went to the kitchen to prepare dinner. After about half an hour, I turned to find W on the kitchen floor behind me. I put her back in the lounge, and twenty minutes later she was in the other room with her sister, who was playing the piano.' W had in fact learned to roll about on the floor to manipulate herself through the lounge, through the door, along the hall and into another room of her choice.

Often it is the anecdotal evidence that makes the difference between raw, objective fact, and an appreciation that the assessment is of a human being, with warmth and potential. Parents are often afraid to add this 'human' perspective, thinking that only rational, objective, quantifiable data is admissible. However, when decisions are being made that will affect a child's whole future life, that child as a person must be considered, not merely the raw data.

Parents need to feel that their understanding and knowledge of their child is important and valued in its own right. Too often, parents feel that their views are sought as a courtesy; the officers, psychologists and teachers are not really seeking additional insight into the child's abilities, difficulties or potential. To elicit this information takes time and also an approach to questioning that may not come naturally to professionals whose training is to 'get the facts'. A typical question of a parent is 'What is X like at home?' This is usually asked after an initial discussion of clinical or assessment findings. Parents' natural reaction to this question is to recount their home experiences that most closely relate to the items discussed immediately before. Thus anecdotes about how a little boy relates to his peers in the cub scout troop, or how a little girl learned to use roller skates, may be lost. And yet it is these anecdotes that can give such a powerful insight into how a child learns, or copes with learning, or interacts with other people.

Until professionals learn to regard this information as being valuable and essential to their understanding of a child, parental evidence, parental contribution and parental involvement will remain an appendix, something to which lip service is paid. Once the power of the extra insight is appreciated, more effective partnerships can be forged, and parents can make a truly positive contribution to the assessment process.

Obstacles to parental partnership

Parents make a raft of assumptions about the way professionals work which impedes the effective involvement of parents as partners. Parents assume that professionals talk to one another, and that when they talk they pass on any important information that the parents may have provided about their child.

The most difficult 'lack of communication' for parents to comprehend is that between teachers within the same school. This is particularly so in primary schools, where there are seldom the vast numbers of staff often found in larger comprehensive secondary schools. Parents assume that teachers discuss a child both formally and informally. In particular, if a parent has had a meeting with the head teacher, they expect that, within a day or so, relevant elements of the content of that discussion will have been passed on to the teacher. Parents expect that what they have said will have been noted, communicated and acted upon. To find that this hasn't happened suggests to the parent that their input was not valued, or that their child's needs are not important. The short-term effects of this are that the parent is annoyed, and may complain openly to the teacher and possibly other parents. The longer-term effects are that the parent will cease to discuss things with the teacher, or headteacher, or SENCO, believing it to be pointless; as a result, the parent will feel increasingly marginalised and uninvolved. The next time someone from the school seeks the involvement of that parent, in a review meeting, or to discuss an incident, the parent's attitude may be negative and uncooperative.

The difficulties of communication between teachers and other members of the education team outside the school are compounded by protocol and procedures, and parents are unhappy when they are exposed to what they perceive to be internal difficulties within the system. Just as parents are frustrated when their comments are not communicated between members of staff within a school, they are also annoyed when important pieces of information are lost between the school and the psychologist, or the psychologist and the LEA officer. This is particularly important during statutory assessment – or Stage Four – when the parent's views are explicitly sought by each professional who assesses the child. When a parent tells a psychologist something, they expect it to be on record, so that the LEA officer will be able to refer to it when drafting the Statement. Too often the information and views given by parents are filtered by the 'receiving professional', and only a summary comment is recorded in the official notes.

Parents are often left in despair of professionals by the additional challenge of communication and mutual understanding between representatives of the different agencies that might be involved. For example, parents assume that, if an occupational or speech and language therapist is visiting their child in school, the school will therefore record the therapist's views. Parents will be extremely irate if this is not done. They are equally annoyed if they find that they have been excluded from important discussions betwen the therapist and the school, or that reports or advice have not been copied to them.

An even greater source of despondency comes when parents have given information to a professional that has not been recorded and so is forgotten when that professional comes to make a decision.

> I couldn't believe it. Here we were, going round looking at special schools, after talking to the officer about which schools to visit, and the officer phones up to say he's trying to put a package of support together for T in mainstream. My husband was fuming. We'd spent a year coming to terms with the idea of special school, discussing it with his current school, speech and language therapist and others, after the psychologist suggested it at the review, and now the officer was going completely the other way.

> (Mrs H, whose son T is now placed at a special language school.)

Professionals dealing with parents need to be sure that they record the content of conversations with parents, as well as any decisions. This has to extend to making adequate notes of all interactions with the parents during informal conversations and formal meetings. In the case quoted above, sufficient information had been given to the school teachers, head teacher, speech and language therapist, educational psychologist and LEA officer over a period of a year to indicate that the parents were willing to consider a special school placement. That change in parental view had not been recorded, so the officer was trying to pull together sufficient resources to support the child in mainstream, thinking that this was consistent with the parents' wishes. The intention was good, but the outcome was a potential disaster.

[When parents approach the assessment process, they often begin with an assumption that they are tapping into an existing partnership among the professionals, with its own efficient and effective communications, mutual understanding and respect. It comes as quite a shock to find that teachers, psychologists, therapists and officers often work completely isolated from each other, and channels of communication are fraught with difficulties of protocol, practical difficulties and politics. These obstacles to efficient working are seldom tolerated by parents, and will not be taken as excuses for inaction.]

Partnership in the wider context

Most of the partnership issues discussed so far refer to the individual case: how a child's parents relate to his or her teachers, the educational psychologist making the assessments, and so on.

A broader application of partnership needs to be mentioned here, for it can affect not only the way in which individual cases are handled, but also the policy and operational framework within which all the professionals work. If used effectively, this wider partnership can work to the advantage of parents and their children, of teachers, psychologists and all other professionals working in the field of special educational needs.

Since 1994, local education authorities have been able to bid for additional funding under the GEST scheme (Grants for Education, Service and Training) to develop parent partnership initiatives. Most have appointed, either on short-term contract or as a permanent post, a Parent Partnership Officer, sometimes known as a Parent Partnership Co-ordinator, or Parent Partnership Adviser. Some LEAs are supporting this post outside the authority, within the voluntary sector, while most have placed the officer within the education department itself.

The brief for the parent partnership initiative varies according to each local education authority, but generally is designed to provide a bridge between parents and the local education authority in the first instance, and possibly facilitate further links with schools and other agencies. They work both on individual cases, to facilitate parents' involvement in the decision-making process about their child, and on a broader basis, developing stronger links between the local education authority and the voluntary sector representing parental interests.

All professionals working within the field of special educational needs should acquaint themselves with the details of their own authority's parent partnership scheme, the name of the officer responsible, and the general remit of the initiative. This will provide the professional with an access point for information about the voluntary sector, and will be a resource to which they can usefully direct parents, so that they can use it directly.

The voluntary sector in general, and parent support groups in particular, have a valuable role to play in advising education authorities on the development of their special educational needs services.

Traditionally, voluntary organisations have been called upon by parents when they feel they need additional support to 'fight' the authority, or school, in order to gain the appropriate provision for their child. The parent support groups are therefore often perceived as aggressive and adversarial, and as such are thought to be very unlikely partners in the constructive debate on developing services and policies.

Most voluntary organisations, however, would prefer to be involved in a proactive way, so that procedures and policies are developed that take into account the 'client' group, and pre-empt many of the possible problems that might be encountered later on. Instead of being left in the position of complaining about issues 'after the event', on a case-by-case basis, they can help ensure that the systems are in place to prevent problems occurring in the first place.

This kind of partnership was introduced in one authority, after parent support groups started getting calls from parents whose children were coming up for secondary transfer. The general complaint was that annual reviews had taken place so long ago that the parents were not fully equipped to make choices about secondary schools. Cases were being tackled one by one, with individual parents fighting for their own child's reviews to be rearranged. By discussion between the voluntary organisations and the LEA, agreement was reached that annual reviews for all children approaching secondary transfer would take place in the term before parents needed to select their preferences. The change required full co-operation from the senior management teams in the LEA, and needed to be brought about as a policy; the result was a reduction in individual cases being fought.

Several local education authorities have set up parent forums where representatives from a range of groups supporting parents meet regularly with officers of the LEA to discuss the way the special educational needs service is delivered, drawing on issues arising from individual cases; they also act as consultative bodies to examine the way the authority's own SEN policy is developed. The 'parent forum' often works alongside other user group consultative bodies such as those drawn from head teachers, SENCOs and governors.

Those LEAs that have initiated such schemes have found that, on the whole, they benefit the authority as much as they do the voluntary sector. The LEA are seen to be accountable directly to their 'client group'; they can address issues without individual cases being raised by name; and they can access a wider network of individuals to monitor the actual delivery of their services. The voluntary organisations find that having access to the authority's representatives on a regular basis and in a businesslike manner enables a positive and constructive exchange of views and information to take place.

Many education authorities invite parent representatives to participate in the work of the education committee and specific working parties examining different aspects of education policy and practice. This can reasonably be extended to sub-committees concerned with special educational needs, where parent representatives have contributions to make regarding the implications of the policies being developed by elected councillors.

Increasingly, education authorities are required to work with other statutory agencies such as social services departments and health authorities. Frequently joint working parties are set up, bringing representatives from each agency to debate joint working practices and inter-agency co-operation. Again, this is a suitable opportunity for parent representatives to be involved. In the field of special educational needs, it is often only the parents who see all of the agencies working with the children, and, as the users of the services, they are often in the best position to point out where weaknesses exist and to make constructive suggestions as to how joint strategies can best be developed.

This approach of involving parents in decisions about issues broader than their own cases can also be usefully extended to schools; this will be considered in the next chapter as part of the discussion about SEN policies.

The Named Person

The Named Person is a specific initiative introduced by the Code of Practice to assist individual parents in the assessment and Statementing process. A Named Person scheme has been operating in Scotland since 1983. At the time of writing this book, the implementation of the Named Person scheme in England and Wales remains rather patchy, with concern being expressed by parents, voluntary organisations and professionals about the implications of the scheme.

The principle is valid, that a child's needs are best identified, assessed and met if the parent's involvement is maximised, and that a parent's involvement will be maximised if they are appropriately helped and supported.

The Named Person is intended to be someone who is independent of the local education authority, who can provide support, impartial information and advice to the parents. The question is 'Who is best suited to perform this role?'

Initially, it was thought that voluntary organisations would take on the role of supplying suitable volunteers who could be trained for the Named Person role. The difficulty for voluntary organisations is that often they are already doing much of this work, but restricting their activities to support and information. The provision of 'advice' has legal connotations that will need to be resolved before the voluntary sector can fully participate in the scheme.

The question of training also raises issues of impartiality. Many education authorities have accepted the responsibility of providing training for Named Person volunteers, through allocation of the funds under the GEST scheme that covers parent partnership. The concern is, however, that if the authority is providing the training, then the information that Named Persons have will be LEA-generated, and therefore not impartial.

In addition, parents are able to identify their own Named Person, who may or may not know anything about the education system or about special educational needs. These additional volunteers will require some training and access to information to enable them to fulfil their role.

Despite these reservations, the principle is accepted by most voluntary organisations and parents. Until the specifics of the Named Person schemes are resolved, it is likely that the voluntary sector will continue to do what it has been doing for years – supporting, befriending and informing parents. What has changed significantly is the acceptance of this activity by LEAs and other education professionals. Parents and befrienders alike welcome the more positive reaction from teachers, head teachers and other professionals to parents bringing with them to meetings a 'friend' who can support them in their participation.

A workable definition of partnership

For a partnership to work, the following conditions should be met:

- Each partner recognises the different skills, experiences and knowledge of each of the other partners;
- Each partner values the skills, experiences and knowledge of each of the other partners;
- All partners recognise the need for the input of each of the partners;
- Each partner feels valued.

Parents do have a different experience; each professional has a different perspective; the parents recognise the need for the input of the professionals. All that remains to make the partnership work is for parents' contribution to be truly valued by the professionals; and for the parents to believe that they are valued.

Practical points

- Remember that parents have more to offer than a repetition of their child's early developmental history.
- Allow parents time and space to participate; they need to be supported so that they gain confidence in their own skills and experience as parents.
- Look for ways to use partnership proactively, to avoid and prevent confrontation developing.
- Encourage organisations as well as individuals to develop the partnership culture.

Table 3.2 Options for partnership

Partner link	Advantages	Disadvantages
Class teacher	Knows parents Knows child	May not know system (especially stages 4 and 5) May be in conflict with parent Unlikely to have access to all other partners Unlikely to know in detail all alternative placements
Head teacher	Knows parents Knows child	May not know system May not have access to all other partners Unlikely to know in detail all alternative placements
SENCO	May know child May know parents Should know system	May not know/have access to all other professionals involved Unlikely to know in detail all alternative placements
Educational psychologist	Knows child Meets parents Should know system May know about all alternative placements	May not have access to all other partners Unlikely to have time to be available to parents in all cases Only involved at stages 3, 4 and 5
LEA officer	Knows about alternative placements Has access to all other professionals Knows system	May not have met parents Unlikely to have met child Unlikely to have time to be available to parents in all cases Only involved at stages 4 and 5
Social worker	If involved, likely to be trusted by parents	Not involved in every case. Unlikely to know educational system in enough detail May not have access to all other partners
Medical officer	Knows child Has met parents	Unlikely to have time to be available to parents in all cases Only involved at stages 4 and 5
Specialist therapist	Knows child Has met parents	Not involved in every case Unlikely to know educational system in enough detail May not have access to all other partners
Independent specialist	Knows child	On outside of system

4   School SEN policies

2:10 – 2:13

By the time this book is published, all maintained mainstream schools will have prepared and published their own individual policies on special educational needs. It is hoped that every single one of these policies includes a sentence about monitoring and review of the policy itself. A policy, if it is to be of any value, must be open to evaluation, its objectives continually reassessed, and its assumptions challenged. For this reason, this chapter concentrates not on how to write the policy – for this will have already been done – but on things to look out for when evaluating that policy, its effectiveness and value. These questions include questions of principle, questions of culture and questions of fact.

Questions of principle

Is SEN considered to be an **additional** *or* **integral** *part of the responsibilities of the school and its governing body?*

For many schools, the introduction of the Code of Practice was seen as an unbearable additional burden on the stretched financial, staffing and emotional resources of their organisations. The requirements of the Code, in terms of staff time and administration, as well as the actual identification and assessment of pupils' special educational needs, combined to impose almost intolerable pressures at a time when teachers were already screaming under the workloads imposed by the National Curriculum. Adding the Code of Practice, while reducing only slightly the National Curriculum under the Dearing review, seemed a cruel irony.

While of course the Code of Practice does add specific responsibilities to the work of schools, the identification of special educational needs, assessment of a child's progress, modification of the teaching style or environment, and involvement of external experts for additional help when required, are all part of what every school should normally be doing in respect of every child. To some observers, it seemed that teachers feared they were suddenly being given an extra and more difficult 20 per cent of pupils, when in fact they had been there all·the time.

The individual support, assessment and development of programmes are not significantly different as a result of the Code of Practice, just more formalised. Following the Code, a child's needs are recognised by a broader audience, which extends beyond the school to those outside the school who are able to identify or provide additional support for any individual child who requires it.

Just as there has been a great move towards integrating pupils with special educational needs into the mainstream environment, so SEN as an issue should be integrated within the entire school philosophy. Unless it is seen as a central strand in the school's ethos, special educational needs provision will always be seen as an additional burden, whereas it should be seen as a means of enhancing what the school offers to all its pupils.

When a child first enters a school, no one can predict whether or not they will, at some later stage, display some learning difficulty. Some children, it is true, can be identified very early, but others may cope and progress for years with no cause for alarm, and then quite unexpectedly experience difficulties with increasingly complex curriculum demands. If SEN is treated as just an additional element of the school's activities, a child's individual special needs may suffer from delayed identification, as he or she is considered part of the 'non-SEN' pupil population. The risk is that no one may be watching for difficulties in these 'normal' children. If SEN is considered a separate element of the school's operation, the risk is increased that, once identified, a child with special educational needs may be seen to be treated differently. This can further increase any anxiety they feel about their difficulties. Other pupils may regard children with special needs as different, and this can exacerbate their feelings of isolation and failure.

If, instead, SEN becomes a normal part of the school's activities, and all staff and all children are kept aware that it is within the normal range of the school's everyday life, there is a smooth transition for both child and staff concerned from non-differentiated curriculum delivery to special provision for each child who needs it.

For the parents, too, the idea that SEN is 'OK' will make a significant difference to their level of confidence in the school's ability to help their child. They will be more open about their concerns, and more receptive to the professionals' approaches to them regarding identification, assessment, provision and review of their child's needs. The risk of the parents feeling isolated within the school community will also be diminished.

Do emotional and behavioural difficulties count as special educational needs, or are they treated differently?

The Code of Practice in particular, and special needs policies in general, identify 'emotional and behavioural difficulties' as a category of special educational need. Certainly when these difficulties become severe, most education authorities and most professionals will acknowledge that 'EBD' is a valid category for provision of specialised school places, in either special schools or special units attached to mainstream schools. In the mainstream, non-Statemented environment, however, the behavioural or anti-social problems exhibited by some children are often treated differently from other types of special educational need. With many children, the first sign that there may be something amiss with their learning is a deterioration in their behaviour. They may become withdrawn or more noticeably disruptive, or display aggressive behaviour. The school's approach to this should be carefully examined not just in the light of any behaviour management policy, but also in the context of its policy regarding special educational needs.

Sadly, many children whose behaviour gives cause for concern are fast-tracked into the sanction, punishment and exclusion route before any purposeful attempts are made to evaluate whether there may be underlying or concomitant learning difficulties. Often these children have to wait until they are in highly specialised EBD provision before anyone tries to look beyond the immediate behavioural difficulties, by which time the emotional turmoil of the child may have become very entrenched and difficult to unravel. An example is given in the box.

> Mrs A was concerned about her son F's transfer to secondary school. He was a bright pupil, who was becoming disruptive in class. He had poor concentration but managed to complete work quickly. Other symptoms suggested other underlying difficulties that should have been examined: poor attention span, resistance to change, difficulties in group situations. His teachers said that he did not warrant even an informal assessment for special needs, because he was bright. However, he would need to be watched carefully, because it was likely that, once in secondary school, he would end up with detentions and maybe even exclusion if his behaviour did not improve. Such a negative prognosis, insensitively delivered, caused extreme anxiety in both the child and the mother about the move to secondary school.

Questions of culture

How involved are parents of children with special needs in the development of the SEN policy?

It is important that the users of the policy, and receivers of the services outlined in the policy, have an opportunity to express their views on the effectiveness of the policy. They should be given the opportunity to suggest ways it can be developed to offer a better service and a more practical range of support for parents and children at the school. In this way, parents become owners of the policy, and will work to help it succeed. As the 'clients' of the service, their views will need to be taken into account.

It is worth considering ways of garnering the parents' opinions on the policy on a regular basis as part of the policy review process. This might be done by questionnaire or by inviting comments during consultations. If there is a parent support group connected to the school, or to a cluster of smaller schools, this may be a useful forum in which parental views can be sought. An open question time should always be included at the AGM, when again the school can be seen to be open about SEN issues.

Does your school have a means of communicating specifically with the parents of children who have SEN, other than during consultations about their own child?

Some special schools have their own parent support group, offering a forum for an exchange of views and experiences among parents and between the parents and staff of the school. In a few larger comprehensive secondary mainstream schools, there are also parent support groups that can achieve some of the same objectives. The isolation of parents described in Chapter 1 is a daily experience, and not confined to the point of identification or diagnosis. In special schools, at least parents are aware that all other parents have children with special needs; even so, it is often difficult for parents to open up to one another if the ice has not been broken already by the school offering group meetings. In mainstream schools, however, the parent of a child with special educational needs can feel doubly isolated, believing that all other parents have no experience or understanding of SEN. The added difficulty of identifying which other parents may share their own experience can add to their reluctance to approach the subject.

As part of the SEN policy of the school, consideration should be given to how the school might enable parents to meet one another, and to meet together with the school, on either a formal or an informal basis, to discuss SEN issues in particular. If such a group has been formed, parents of newly identified children can be referred to this group, or individual members of the group, for information and support, to help them accept the fact of their own child's difficulties and understand how their child's needs might be met and how to avoid their feeling 'stigmatised'.

Even if such a formal group is thought inappropriate in any one particular school, it is worth asking individual parents of children with special educational needs whether they might act as a contact point for new parents. Referral of parents to other parents can have direct benefits for the staff of a school; it can be used to 'delegate' some of the initial information-gathering; and it can offer an opportunity for new parents to gain confidence in the school's ability to meet their child's needs by discussing their own child's difficulties with a parent whose child's needs are already being met. Well-informed parents can be tremendous allies to the school, and can help new parents understand the roles of the different teaching and support staff, and of external advisers such as educational psychologists, on a much more informal basis than perhaps is possible for the SENCO or head teacher.

How does the school encourage parents to use outside help?

Many schools are nervous of parents who want to bring along 'a friend' to a meeting. Head teachers and teachers are suspicious of Named Persons being involved when a child has a Statement or is undergoing assessment. Again, the Parent Partnership Officer may be able to offer advice. It may be worth establishing links with the voluntary organisations from which many Named Persons are drawn, to discuss openly concerns about the role of befrienders so that a few ground rules can be agreed between all the parties.

Has the school sought parents' views on what information they would like to see reported at the AGM?

While there are clearly a few obligatory items in the SEN report at the AGM, there may be some issues which parents themselves would like to see mentioned. If contact has already been established with the parents of children with special educational needs, it should be possible to find out what they would like to know.

Does the school have a policy of integration of children from special schools or units?

For many children placed in special schools or units, reintegration is a major objective. A period of time in a specialist environment is often felt sufficient to equip that child for reintegration. However, a barrier to this progress is often the reluctance of a mainstream school to accept such pupils, even with the additional support they often bring as a result of their Statement. In addition, some children in special schools benefit from exposure to a mainstream environment, even if they cannot make use of this provision on a full-time basis. Specific links with local special schools may open avenues to explore in this regard.

What are the links between the pastoral and SEN systems within the school?

This is often particularly important in large comprehensive secondary schools. A pupil with special needs can often feel lost in a community of a thousand-plus pupils, and the additional support required may not necessarily involve only the SENCO or learning support staff. A positive pastoral and welfare system may be sufficient to support that pupil in the general day-to-day activities around the school. Consideration might also be given to including a system of older pupils acting as mentors to younger pupils on a general basis, into which children with special needs can be integrated. Again, this avoids the danger of such children feeling that they are being treated 'differently', and can serve to advertise the generally positive nature and ethos of the school as a whole.

Is the complaints procedure for SEN clear and accessible? Has it been used by parents?

A quantitative analysis of the usage of any complaints procedure is a measure not just of the level of complaints about the school's SEN policy or practice, but also of the procedure's accessibility, and how much parents trust its impartiality. An initial increase in the number of complaints in itself may not be cause for concern, but conversely may be a cause for celebration; it means that parents are feeling more comfortable about airing their views; it means that the school can develop its SEN policy and practice in the light of real experience; and it is likely to mean that parents are complaining earlier, before their positions and those of the school become entrenched.

What provision is there for children whose home language is not English?

If there is a significant proportion of children or parents at the school for whom English is not the first language, is the SEN policy available in other languages, or in Braille or on tape? (The RNIB – see Appendix B – can advise about transcription services into and from Braille.) Are there facilities within the school for interpretation or for bilingual support to help parents use the SEN service and complaints procedures? Are links made with the multicultural support services in the local education authority in order to access interpreter and translation services for parents?

What is the reality of integration for pupils with difficulties?

Is this handled sensitively? While schools are encouraged to help children with special needs participate in as wide a range of the school's activities as possible, there can sometimes be too rigid an interpretation of this.

> In Y2 the teacher insisted my daughter ran in a sports day sprint knowing full well she would be – to everyone's discomfort – a fortnight behind the others. I was told, 'If she's in a normal school she has to be treated as a normal child'!

(Mrs J whose daughter has dyspraxia.)

Questions of fact

Does the 'designated governor' have any experience of SEN?

SEN is a complex issue, as complex as curriculum development and financial management. The regulatory and administrative frameworks that are involved, particularly since the 1993 Education Act and its Code of Practice, make it a potential minefield. The staff in a school responsible for delivery of SEN services – particularly the SENCO – need to be sure that they have access to at least one governor who does not need every element explaining from scratch, and who can offer specific guidance and direction as well as support and encouragement.

While there are many courses available, through the National Association of Governors and Managers (NAGM) and through LEAs themselves, to help governors to gain increased knowledge and awareness of SEN issues, it can be useful to start by designating a governor who already has an interest in, or experience of, special needs. In many schools, the governor designated for responsibility for special educational needs may be a parent governor who has a child with special educational needs. The school might also consider approaching local voluntary organisations for suitable candidates to co-opt for this post.

As previous chapters have shown, the day-to-day pressures on a parent of a child with special educational needs may mean that the SEN parent governor cannot always offer the time or emotional resource needed to take on this specific responsibility without considerable assistance. There is also a risk that an individual parent may extrapolate from their own experience to the more general SEN situation, diverting attention specifically to their own child's type of special needs. However, if these are the risks, they are far outweighed by the fact that this governor will have empathy for other parents of children with special needs, and provide a useful and usable conduit for channelling the expression of concerns and opinions into the governing body as a whole. Other parents may find this governor more approachable than a designated governor without direct personal experience of special educational needs.

In some schools, the designated governor may be someone who has no direct personal experience of SEN. This need not bar them from taking on the role, but part of their specific training and development should include an opportunity to meet with parents of children in the school who have special needs of different types. Openness and accessibility are key objectives for the designated governor if the school's SEN policy is to develop fully.

Is the designated governor the only governor with interest in, or experience of, SEN?

As with many other jobs within the governing body, it is important that the SEN governor is not isolated, that other governors have an understanding of the general issues surrounding SEN, and can act as deputies or assistants in carrying out the specific duties of the SEN governor. Particularly if the designated governor is a parent of a special needs child, there may be times when additional personal support from a fellow governor will be especially important in helping that parent sustain their active involvement.

To whom is the SEN policy distributed as a matter of course?

The Code of Practice suggests that the SEN policy be given to parents when their child is first identified as having, or likely to have, special educational needs. It is also to be made available to any parent who requests a copy. These two opportunities are important, as the parents receiving it will be ready to receive it, and are likely to be actively seeking information and help.

However, consideration should be given to circulating the policy document along with other information on a general, routine basis, firstly to all parents with children at the school, and secondly to all parents considering applying for a place at the school for their child.

By being circulated in this way, the information will be available to parents who are concerned about their child, but who may not yet have expressed that concern openly to their child's teachers. They will be reassured that their concerns will be taken seriously, and that there is a network of support available within the school to help them and their child. It also acts as a signal to parents throughout the school that SEN is an accepted part of the everyday life of the school. Parents whose children do not have special needs will see that other children having difficulties, of whatever sort, are accepted within the school alongside their own children, and should not be kept hidden or avoided.

For new parents, it will help complete the wider picture of the school, its caring and pastoral philosophy inextricably wound into the overall life of the school.

In addition, as SEN is to be newly reported on at the AGM from September 1995, it would be helpful if, at least for the first few years, a summary of the SEN policy were included in the papers alongside the report reviewing the policy's implementation. SEN must be seen to be firmly on the school's agenda.

How does your school link with the voluntary organisations in its area?

Voluntary organisations are usually keen to make links with schools, but the sheer number of schools in any catchment area is high, and time and other resources within the voluntary groups are very restricted. This constrains them from proactively building working relationships. It may be worth considering that individual representatives from the school, such as the designated governor, or the SENCO, attend meetings of the voluntary organisations in the area to meet with the volunteers involved. By taking out membership, they will be able to receive notification of meetings, and be included on circulation for newsletters and other information. Voluntary organisations are often very useful sources of information for professionals as well as for parents, and the two-way link will be appreciated by the organisers.

By getting to know the groups in more detail, and making personal contact, a school will be better placed to offer relevant information to parents during Stages One to Three of assessment.

Has your school made contact with the Parent Partnership Officer in the LEA?

Many LEAs have been able to set up parent partnership schemes, under the initial impetus of GEST funding. Although in some authorities, these are time-limited contractual appointments, considerable amounts of work have nevertheless been done by these officers in order to establish links with parent support groups and other voluntary organisations on an authority-wide basis. They may also know about linking opportunities with other agencies, such as social services, health authorities and so on, which can be of assistance both to parents of children in your school, and to staff such as the SENCO and learning support team.

What contacts does your mainstream school have with any special schools or special units in your area?

While outreach is offered on a formal basis in some parts of the country, and for some types of special provision, in other areas this is left to a much more informal agglomeration arrangement involving loose clusters of schools. The teaching and support staff within special schools and units have a tremendous amount of very practical experience to offer their mainstream colleagues. Too often, this informal network of inter-professional advice and support is overlooked, as mainstream colleagues mix only with other mainstream staff, and special school staff mix only with their special sector colleagues. Although this is primarily a matter of inter-professional support, the indirect benefits of mainstream and special sector staff mixing can also accrue to parents, who can begin to see that the two sectors are but different parts of a whole system, instead of entirely separate worlds. This is particularly important if a parent might have to begin to consider the possibility of special school for their own child. Meeting a blank expression on the face of the teacher, head teacher or SENCO at the mention of 'special school' can be enough to increase exponentially the anxiety already felt by a parent whose child is undergoing assessment or a review of placement.

The benefits also accrue to the children. Staff preparing children for reintegration from special schools need to be fully aware of the way mainstream schools operate, to gear their pre-transfer support accordingly. They should be able to give the child realistic expectations of what will be required of them in their new environment.

Parent partnership policies for special schools

A parent whose child attends a special school may feel very isolated. They are already 'different' from the other parents in their community, by the fact that their child goes to a different type of school. Common ground in parenting is lost. The added difficulty of distance and loss of community with other parents of children in the special school makes them especially vulnerable.

Quite often, their child will travel some distance to attend the special school, and may be transported in a taxi or school bus, so that the parents do not have daily contact with the school and its staff, or with other parents.

Specific efforts should be made to ensure that parents of children at a special school feel part of a community, for mutual support and for ease of communication between school and parents.

This may also be useful for prospective parents visiting the school. Parents of children already at the school may be encouraged to offer a contact service where prospective and new parents can talk to other parents about the school, and about the feelings they experience because their child is no longer part of the mainstream.

5 Stages One and Two – coping within school

The early signs that something may be amiss with a child's progress can generate a strange mixture of reactions in parents. Just as with diagnosis of significant handicap or impairment, the response includes anger, denial and hope. The degree of response may be different (although this is not necessarily the case) but teachers should be aware that, in any rational response from the parents, these feelings will also be present.

There is a delicate balance to be struck, between confirming the seriousness of the situation, and emphasising the mildness of the learning difficulty identified. The fact that a child is experiencing sufficient difficulty to register even at Stage One or Stage Two means that the child does have special educational needs. That the difficulty is not considered sufficiently severe to warrant a higher degree of intervention should be a reassurance to parents.

This chapter seeks to examine the relationship issues between parents and schools for Stages One and Two. It is recognised that some schools may not have separate stages at this level, which is why these two stages are included in one chapter. At both of these two stages, the school will operate using its own resources and expertise almost exclusively in identifying and meeting the special educational needs of children. This means that the relationships in which parents are involved are largely limited to school staff. The partnerships should be developmental, based on pre-existing relationships between the parent, teachers, SENCO and head teacher. No new players are likely to be involved. Parents' trust and faith in the professionals whom they meet, and in the system as a whole, can stand or fall according to the relationship developed in the early stages of identification and assessment.

His first school did not/could not understand his difficulties and he became withdrawn and uncooperative in class, and did not appear to be learning anything. I was unhappy with the way the head and the class teacher spoke to me and my son. They did not seem to listen to me ... At the new school his first class teacher was like an angel from heaven. She came to a dyspraxia conference with me and understood. She has passed on her understanding throughout the other teachers and children. She was a very experienced teacher, with over thirty years of teaching...

(A parent on his dyspraxic son.)

Stage One and Two trigger: concern expressed by the parent

2:71 and 2:86

Only a small minority of parents will understand the National Curriculum, its levels and key stages, attainment targets and so on. Parents of children attending school now will have experienced quite a different educational system from the one that their children are subject to. Therefore, it is reasonable to suggest that most parents may not know what to expect of their child at different levels and stages within the National Curriculum. This does not mean that they are unable to evaluate in general terms their child's progress; neither does it mean that they are unable to identify specific elements within their child's achievements that are below reasonable expectations.

Where the child has older siblings, the parents will have a reasonably clear idea of what the older brothers or sisters were able to do at a similar age. Most parents will be able to see what other children are achieving: by looking at the displays on the walls in the classroom when they collect their child from primary school; by talking to other parents; by looking at examples of work on open days. From this evidence they may begin to compare their own child's progress, and begin to be concerned. It may be that the child has also expressed anxiety about new pieces of work they are finding difficult.

Parents rarely express their concern when they first feel it. A mother or father might notice something in their child's work, or relationship with other children, or attitude to school, and merely store it in the back of their minds. They will then look for further signs that might confirm or contradict their initial view. This may take place over several weeks or even months, and may not even be discussed privately with the other parent, a grandparent, or friend. Sometimes they might carefully question their child about the work they are doing, or about the other children in their class, but this may be inconclusive.

An appointment at a parent consultation evening may be the first opportunity for the parent to mention anything about their concerns. Many parents are nervous of these occasions, even though teachers make every effort to keep them as informal as possible. Parents are aware that they have a limited amount of time, and that the teacher will be giving them important information about their child's work. They will be conscious that other parents may be within earshot, anxious for their own appointments, and getting restless if there is a delay. Under such circumstances, parents are already feeling pressurised, and may want to express their concern about their child, but not know how to talk about their worries, or how to express themselves.

Teachers often underestimate what the parent has gone through to get as far as a simple expression of concern. For example, the parent's simple statement 'What about his reading? I think he's not finding it easy' may reflect nights of worry and anxiety as the parents have tried to help their child read. The innocent question 'How does he get on with the other children in the class?' can be an expression of deep anxiety about their child's apparent lack of friends, or difficulties in forming relationships. This highlights another issue that should be borne in mind. Often the parents will raise their concerns in a rather oblique way, and the area of their child's progress that they initially identify to the teacher as cause for concern may not actually be the real underlying worry.

An analogous situation might be a woman who makes an appointment with her doctor. On being asked what her concern is, she might say, 'I think I've found a lump.' What she is really thinking, however, is 'I think I might have cancer.' In this case, the direct expression of concern is considerably less weighty than the patient's actual state of mind. So it is with parents asking about their children's progress.

The pressure of the parent consultation appointment, then, sometimes serves to diminish the response from the teacher. It might be that the parents have only managed to raise their concerns at the very end of their appointment. The teacher is getting ready to meet the next set of parents, and may be looking at the clock, conscious of the accumulated delays encountered through the consultation session. The teacher may be feeling very tired. Under these circumstances, the teacher may respond in such a way as to artificially curtail the ensuing discussion. This can result in the parents thinking either that their concerns are unjustified, or that the teacher does not take them seriously. It is important, therefore, that teachers prepare a strategy prior to any parent consultation session for dealing with such occurrences. Staff should decide in advance whether the head teacher might be available to talk to parents who are concerned, or whether specific follow-up appointments will be offered to discuss the concern in more detail within the next few days. Perhaps the SENCO might be available to review the parents' feelings and any supporting evidence. Whatever the strategy, it must ensure that the parents get a full opportunity to explain their concerns when both they and the teacher are not under pressure of time.

A common response to parents who express initial concerns that teachers themselves have not identified is immediate reassurance. Parents are told there is 'nothing to worry about', or that 'there are others in the class who are further behind'. Very often, these attempts at reassurance serve only to obscure the concern, or to anger the parents. They may feel that their concerns are not taken seriously enough if they only receive a quick comment aimed at reducing their concern. Even more annoying is

68

when parents take trouble and time to explain their child's difficulties to each new teacher, only to find that the information is disregarded.

> We had explained to every new teacher and at each change of school ... that O was slow to read and had great difficulty with spelling and yet they either 'hadn't noticed' or 'found it irritating that she came to ask for spellings so often'.
>
> (Mrs L, whose daughter O has specific learning difficulties.)

Parents are often very keen to believe that there is nothing wrong with their child. This is particularly so where they have raised their concerns for the first time. Any response from the teacher that reassures them, or diverts their concern, will probably be accepted initially with a sigh of relief, resulting in the parents failing to follow through. When they subsequently have cause to resurrect their concerns, perhaps in later years, after seeing further deterioration in their child's attitude to school or in their performance, they may resent the early reassurances that they were given, and come to mistrust the opinions of professionals.

2:72 – 2:74

Stage One in the Code of Practice does require that any expression of concern meets with an acknowledgement, at least, and an investigation of the concern so that a fair and realistic picture of the child's abilities can be compiled.

Parents are rarely concerned unnecessarily. Many may not be able to express the nature of their concern in 'educational' terms, and certainly very few would be able to use National Curriculum jargon; but if a parent is concerned, it is the duty of any professional to take those concerns seriously, and to be seen to be taking them seriously. If the parents' expectations of their child are unrealistic (such as expecting a five-year-old to write an essay), then the review process of Stage One can be used to help the parents understand the realistic achievement levels for their child. In this way, teachers can ensure that parents are not placing their child under undue pressure to achieve at home, and are not likely to give unnecessary negative feedback to their child for achieving at what is really an acceptable level. Unreasonable parental pressure to achieve might lead to a child developing low self-confidence and esteem, and undermining the acceptable level of performance that they are achieving. Care should be taken, however, to avoid suppressing expectations for a child who is inherently able, but whose SEN may need addressing.

Parental expectations, and parental concerns, are rarely set against the class peer group. There is a problem in some schools where overall achievement levels are lower than, say, in another school of a similar type.

There may be a greater proportion of children with special needs, leading to a generally lower 'average' being achieved. The individual child's achievements must not be gauged only against the 'average' available in the class, or even in the school. Concerns that a child is underachieving in their own right should be addressed.

3:51 (ii)

The Code of Practice does allow for this at Stage Four; a child may be considered to have special educational needs if they are achieving at a lower level than they are expected to achieve. This is irrespective of the peer group. The principle is sound for Stages One to Three also. Parents are particularly good at identifying their child as 'bright' but not achieving. Concerns of this nature need to be taken as seriously as concerns about a child who is falling behind his or her peer group.

Stage One and Two Trigger: concern expressed by the teacher

By the time a teacher expresses concern to a child's parents, it is likely that some work will already have been done to investigate the difficulties and possibly to differentiate the teaching in the classroom. There may have been discussions among different members of staff, particularly if more than one teacher is involved with a child.

2:72 and 2:85

The Code of Practice advises that the parents should be consulted. The question arises: how and when might be the most suitable opportunities for this consultation to take place?

It is inappropriate to wait for an open parent consultation evening to express these concerns to the parents if this might result in unnecessary delay. For all the reasons outlined above, the parent consultation is a pressurised situation, in terms both of time and of environment. Even if the child's identified special educational need is relatively minor, the parents do need time and explanation to understand the nature of the difficulty their child is experiencing, and time to discuss its implications. It is possible that only one parent will be present during this initial discussion, and they may need extra help to confirm the details so that they can communicate accurately with their partner. They will want to discuss with the teacher how best to help their child, or how to discuss the difficulties with the child. In particular, parents whose child is displaying emotional and behavioural difficulties require a more sensitive handling than can be achieved in open parent consultations.

We endured open parents' evenings which we felt extremely damaging emotionally both to us and our child, escalating his problems throughout the community. Teachers must become more sensitive to the needs of parents and children and not sensationalise their situation.

(Mr and Mrs G, commenting on a primary school's response to their son W, who displayed significant behavioural difficulties, but whose learning difficulties were not fully recognised until he was fifteen.)

For the same reasons, it may be inappropriate to address the issue in the informal period at the end of the school day when the parent is collecting the child from school. Parents usually have a limited amount of time available in these circumstances, and will not be prepared for such a discussion. In addition, the way information is communicated in this informal setting may be detrimental to parental co-operation, when the child may be within hearing, as well as other children from the class, and other parents.

The classroom teacher called us, his parents, to see her and in full presence and hearing of the child (then eight years old) said that he was disruptive, lazy, slow and not concentrating or staying on task. He would not remember things he was taught and was in her opinion a 'bone head'. This meeting was the start of our investigations.

(Mr P, whose son has developmental motor learning difficulties.)

Wherever possible an appointment should be made when the teacher and the parents can spend time discussing the child's special educational needs in detail.

Parents' reactions to the news that their child is having difficulties will range from gratitude to denial. They may say, 'Yes, I am concerned too. Thank you for noticing. What can we do to help?'; or they may respond, 'There's nothing wrong with my child, it must be the way you are teaching her (him).' Either way, time and space are required to discuss the matter reasonably and calmly.

There is, of course, a third reaction from parents. This can be called apparent indifference. Some parents will state quite clearly that they expect the teacher to sort the problem out, and that if the child is having difficulties in class, it is the class teacher's responsibility to deal with the situation. However, for some parents, the suggestion that their child is having difficulties may result in a mental block. Apparent indifference does not mean that they do not care, or do not want to help. They just need more time to come to terms with the fact, and prepare themselves to offer help.

Full consultation with and involvement of the parents at these early stages will help to build a working partnership that can sustain through more significant intervention later on, should that prove necessary. If parents are allowed to remain remote from their child's difficulties and support at this stage, they will feel ill-equipped to offer support to their child later. Conversely, if the intervention at Stage One or Stage Two succeeds in helping the child overcome their special educational needs, then the parents' confidence will be boosted as a result of being involved in the successful outcome.

Stage One and Stage Two are not isolated processes. They may represent the only special intervention a child needs, but they can still serve as a means to consolidate the partnership between home and school for the rest of that child's school life. It may lead to further, more intensive intervention at Stage Three and beyond. Again, the parents' involvement in their child's education under these circumstances will be very important for their child's chances of success. Stages One and Two present an opportunity, at a time of relatively low pressure and stress, for parents to gain confidence in their ability to participate in assessment and provision; a new skill that may be required later.

If the initial concern expressed by a teacher relates to the child's behaviour or emotional state, parents are very likely to feel that they are being blamed for their child's difficulties. Unlike most other special educational needs, emotional and behavioural difficulties are often believed to be 'caused' by external influences in the child's life. The most important influence in the child's life is the home and his or her parents. Therefore, runs the argument, difficulties in a child's behaviour must stem from something in the home or in the way the parents deal with the child.

One of the first questions asked by teachers when a child presents with difficult behaviour is frequently: 'Is there anything happening at home that might be upsetting him/her?' By asking this question, the teacher appears to be implying that it is something in the home that is responsible for difficulties with the child in school. This may not be the intention behind the question, but is often perceived as such. Although teachers should be encouraged to identify any and all factors in the child's circumstances that might be affecting his or her performance or behaviour, the way this question is asked can mean the difference between encouraging partnership and engendering hostility.

Subject to this line of questioning, many parents begin to feel that they are being judged, instead of their child's needs being evaluated.

> I felt as if I was in the dock. Every question seemed to imply that my marriage was under review, the way I brought my children up was under question, the fact that I go out to work was being condemned. They wanted to apportion blame, and they wanted to apportion it to me. They never looked at what they were doing to see if that was causing his bad behaviour. I felt persecuted.

(Mrs J, about her son V, who presented with difficult behaviour.)

The apparent or perceived condemnation can also apply where the child's difficulties are in the area of language or reading development. A simple enquiry about whether or not the parents read with the child at home can be interpreted as an implied criticism for not doing so. For a child with delayed language development, there may be an implication that the parents did not talk to him or her enough at the toddler stage.

Conversely, a supportive school can help parents when the problems are encountered at home rather than in school.

> The school have been very helpful, understanding and supportive through all of my son's difficulties ... My son's behaviour in school is fine, he tends to let off steam when he's at home. When I just went to school concerning his behaviour at home, they had a shock because in general they felt he was a very easy-going child, but now they are aware of the situation at home and they are very helpful and help work out strategies to help us all cope with his problem.

> (Mrs J, whose son has dyslexia.)

Stages One and Two: information for parents

It is useful at these very early stages to offer parents as much information as they may need to understand their child's difficulties, to help determine and implement any special provision and to identify sources of personal support and assistance.

The following is a simple checklist of information that might be useful to give out at this stage:

- The school's SEN policy, including the name of the SENCO.
- Any information available from the local education authority that might be useful; for example, literature about the LEA's SEN policy and information about any parent partnership schemes.
- Information about voluntary organisations or parent support groups that might be able to help with specific types of learning difficulties.
- Sources of additional assessment, for example, for speech and language difficulties, sensory impairments or behaviour difficulties.
- Explanation of the term 'Special Educational Needs', including (if available) a copy of the Department for Education booklet: 'Special educational needs – a guide for parents'.

Stage One: the provision

Parents may be keen to be involved in the provision to meet their child's Stage One special educational needs. Help with reading, or with homework generally, may require, not just *more* input from parents, but a different approach. Expectations of the amount of work a child might be asked to complete may differ during the Stage One phase. Attitudes to success and ways to identify lack of success may need to vary according to the needs identified. Although there may not be a specific, written plan, teachers should take time to help parents understand what is being expected of their child, so that they can encourage achievement and praise success.

It is also important for parents to be aware of any differentiation taking place in the classroom. Envisage a situation where a child with special educational needs is not being asked to write a story about a television programme they have seen, although the rest of the class is to do so. Parents talk to each other at the end of the school day, and it is important that neither the parent nor the child with the special educational needs is made to feel different from his or her peers in front of them. If they are, both child and parent can come to feel embarrassed about the child's difficulties, and this may begin a process of isolation that is very hard to break once started.

Stage One: review

2:82 – 2:84

The first review of the child's Stage One special educational needs will be an important opportunity to discuss with the parents the nature of their child's difficulties, if they have not been able to be involved hitherto.

If at all possible, the parents should be invited to the review of their child's Stage One progress. If there is good news, sharing it will benefit the working relationship between school and home. In particular, if parents are unable to see their child's teacher informally at the end of the school day, it may be the only opportunity for the teacher to hear what progress is being made at home.

If there are continuing concerns, it is important that all parties are agreed on the next plan of action. If further intervention is required, at Stage Two or Stage Three, or if early referral for statutory assessment is required, the parents need to be able to work closely with all the professionals they encounter, and the teachers and support staff in the school will initially form the nucleus of that partnership.

Stage Two: the provision

2:93

The Code of Practice requires schools to produce an Individual Education Plan (IEP) when a child is identified as being at Stage Two. It is important that this IEP clearly states every individual need that has been identified, and how each of those needs is to be met. The IEP is important for two reasons: to ensure that everyone involved in teaching and supporting the child has a basis from which to work, within overall agreed strategies throughout the school and across the curriculum; and to ensure that the parents are fully informed of the whole range of support their child is receiving.

As with the more formal Statement of Special Educational Needs, any particular strengths that have been identified should be included, as well as those areas where the child's abilities are within the average of his or her peers. This will both allow staff to use the child's relatively strong areas to help overcome weaknesses, and form a baseline from which progress can be made. In addition, it is particularly helpful for parents to have the good news about their child's performance, as well as any that is less good. Too often, discussion of special needs, even at these relatively mild to moderate levels, concentrates on the difficulties, and parents are left feeling very despondent about their child's future prospects. This can add to a lack of confidence in their own abilities as parents. A balanced, open and honest discussion of successes and limitations is the most appropriate way to proceed.

If at all possible, it is helpful if the parents can meet with the SENCO and class or form tutor to discuss the plan, preferably while it is being developed, but at the very least once it has been written. If new staff are to be involved with the child in the provision of additional support, it is helpful for parents if the opportunity is taken to introduce the new staff member, either face to face, or at least by description. This is particularly important where the child is not able or willing to explain to his or her parents what is going on at school, and may just mention a new staff member, without being able to explain their role. It helps to cement the partnership of support between home and school.

If any particular teaching strategies or schemes are to be used, it is helpful if these are explained to the parents in a way that the parents can understand. It is unlikely that many parents will be very familiar with particular reading schemes, for example, and time spent explaining these at the start will save misunderstandings later on.

Parents who are able and willing to offer support at home should be encouraged, through the IEP, to continue that support. It may be, however, that the particular involvement at home can concentrate on the non-academic aspects of the child's special needs, particularly supporting development of good social relationships, or nurturing self-esteem and self-confidence. Discussions with parents about expectations regarding homework are particularly important, as parents may not understand what is an acceptable level of work. It will be important to include here any special arrangements for home/school communication, so that immediate feedback can be provided if necessary.

> It was an absolute nightmare. We had agreed to look at his homework diary each evening so we could make sure he did it. But I couldn't understand the questions, so couldn't help him. We ended up having a row about it. What should have taken half an hour ended up taking all evening, and it still wasn't finished by the time he went to bed. I tried phoning the Learning Support Teacher the next day, but by the time I'd got through to her, he'd already got into trouble about not doing the homework properly.
>
> (Mrs L, regarding her son W who has specific learning difficulties and receptive language difficulties.)

For children who have been failing for some time, or whose self-confidence is affected by their difficulties, their relationships with their peer group and even with the staff may have deteriorated, and non-educational 'pastoral' support may be needed to help the child overcome the risk of being isolated or coming into conflict with others in the school. It is important that pastoral and SEN staff within the school work together to provide consistent support for the child.

> We learned that E had been put on a programme of social isolation because of a couple of incidents of fighting. He had to spend breaks alone and was not allowed to sit with the others at registration. When we had a review with the SENCO, we found out that she had not been consulted about this. It set him back horribly: part of his problem was difficulty relating to his peer group, and yet here was institutionalised segregation – almost humiliation – which all the SEN support was trying to overcome.
>
> (Mr K, whose son E has specific learning difficulties and emotional difficulties.)

The way the school proposes to monitor progress and review targets should also be clear in the IEP. These should not merely be quantitative measures of reading, spelling or other academic tasks, although these need to be included where appropriate. Again, parental involvement can be valuable. The parents in particular will be able to monitor certain qualitative parameters, for example: ease and willingness with which homework has been tackled; willingness to talk about school when the child gets home; reduction in anxiety about to going to school.

Parents should be invited to the IEP review, and the date and time of the review should be set in consultation with them.

Stage Two: review

2:96

Again, the review is an opportunity to emphasise the positive as well as identify any continuing or progressive difficulties. By involving the parents, the decisions that may need to be made following the review can be agreed by all parties.

When determining whether or not a child can revert to Stage One or no longer needs special help, it is important to ensure that the parents understand that withdrawal of extra help will not adversely affect their child's further progress. Parents are often unwilling to see support reduced, in fear that their child may then revert to failure. This is where care in drawing up the initial IEP pays off. Where individual needs and matching provision have been identified in the Plan, it will be easier to identify those elements of support that are no longer needed, and back this up with evidence of success.

A decision to continue at Stage Two does not necessarily mean 'more of the same', and may result in an amended IEP. Again, it is important that staff help parents understand the difference between an escalation of provision and a decision not to move the child on to Stage Three. This is an excellent opportunity to discuss the nature of Stage Three with parents, so that they can be aware of future options. It is useful to explain at this time the criteria the school will use to determine whether Stage Three might be required.

If the decision is made, at the Stage Two review, that the child needs to move to Stage Three, it is important for the SENCO or other member of staff to take time to explain in some detail to the parents what Stage Three involves. This is especially important in respect of the likely 'external specialist' that the school will call on. As the next chapter shows, this can often be a daunting development for parents.

Once the review meeting has taken place, any new IEP, or a decision to change stages, and the reasons for that decision, should be sent to the parents in writing. Where the parents are unable to attend the review, it is important that they are advised of the outcome of the review, preferably in writing as well as orally, and preferably not as the parents call to collect the child at the end of the school day. A relevant member of staff should make themselves available to the parents for a follow-up discussion. This might be the SENCO or form tutor or class teacher, but must be someone who has been actively involved in the review.

Practical points

- *Teachers*: If you have identified a learning difficulty, or behavioural difficulty, in a child, consider carefully how and when to discuss this with the parents.

  Allow parents time to understand what you are saying about their child's difficulties: how severe they might be; what is being done in school to address the problems.

If you question the parents about what factors at home may be affecting the child's school performance, be sure to emphasise what investigations are also being carried out in school.

Involve parents as much as possible in the planning and review processes for Stages One and Two.

- *SENCOs:* For a child at Stage Two, take time to explain your role to the parents. Involve the parents in the development of the IEP, and make sure they have a copy. Invite the parents to the review.
- *Head teachers:* Be available for parents who may be concerned about the school's overall strategy for their child.
- *Governors:* Be aware of children who are at Stages One and Two. Identify the resources that are being applied to support their needs. Be prepared to support the school's budgeting for special needs in the light of actual needs identified on the SEN register.

6   Stage Three – involving others

The key characteristic of Stage Three is the involvement of one or more external specialists to provide advice and support to help the pupil make progress. The widening of the partnership can be a difficult time for parents, but if good working relationships have been developed over previous stages, or in the decision to involve external advisers, then most parents will welcome that extension.

However, some parents may feel that this development should have been initiated sooner. If a child has a history of difficulties that strategies at Stage One and/or Stage Two have not overcome, the parents may resent the apparent delay in accessing expert help. In many cases, this may be a reasonable criticism. There is limited availability of educational psychology time and of specialist advisory teachers from LEA central support services or outreach departments of special schools. Parents may have the impression that their child has been held back from Stage Three because of that limitation, rather than because their child's needs did not warrant going on. Parents are often told that there is a very long waiting list of children who are being referred to the educational psychologist, and that 'there are other children with greater needs' who are ahead of their own child on that list. Given this information, parents may acquiesce, being sympathetic with the school's plight; or they might become angry at the apparent trivialisation of their own child's difficulties. Parents are interested only in their child's needs; introducing issues relating to other children is seldom a useful strategy.

It may be helpful to identify children early in their Stage Two progress who might require subsequent referral to external advisers and specialists. Thus the 'waiting list' can act as a prediction and planning tool, including the Stage Two children with likely future needs. This process of predictive audit can help considerably in developing the LEA's policy for allocating central support resources to schools in future years, as it provides a factual basis for identifying the needs of individual schools and of the LEA as a whole. Many local education authorities ration psychology and other services on a basis of assumed need, because firmer data are not available. The data to determine true demand only exist in schools, and therefore the onus is on schools to begin to develop the database that can facilitate a more appropriate allocation of these central resources.

Introducing the new team member(s)

Parents may need time to come to terms with the fact that their child needs yet more specialised help. It is essential that when the involvement of external specialists is proposed, the parents are given time to understand the role of these individuals, and how they might be able to help. This is especially important in the case of the educational psychologist.

For many parents, a suggestion that their child be seen by 'the psychologist' is a frightening idea. Those unfamiliar with the background, specialisation and expertise of an educational psychologist may have unfounded but real fears. To them, 'psychologist' means that there is something fundamentally wrong with their child, that it is the child's mental state that is being questioned, and by inference, their own performance as parents. 'Psychologist', to the uninitiated, is indistinguishable from 'psychiatrist' or 'psychoanalyst'.

The member of school staff (probably the SENCO) who first proposes the psychologist's involvement, should stress the *educational* element of the title, and then proceed to explain their role. It is helpful if the authority's psychology service can produce a leaflet explaining the role of the psychologist. If one is available, a copy should be given to the parents. Such a leaflet should explain, in easily understood language: who the educational psychologist is – both in general terms and, if possible, by name; what their involvement might be; how they conduct their assessment; how parents can contact them; what their ongoing involvement might be; how they will report back to the parents and the school; the rights of the parent to be informed of the date, time and place of the assessment; and the parents' rights to be present during any assessment. If no such leaflet is available, the school might consider producing one of their own, perhaps as an appendix to the school's SEN policy statement.

Parents should always be informed of the date and time of any assessments to be carried out by any external adviser or specialist. This is for several reasons. Firstly, they will then be able, if appropriate, to advise their child in advance that this particular individual will be coming in to school to see them. Secondly, they will not be alarmed when their child comes home from school and reports that they have been to see someone different. Thirdly, parents have a right to know who is seeing their child, when and why. Parents also have a right to be present when their child is being assessed or examined, although this should be discussed with the parents beforehand.

Where specialist advisory teachers are to be involved, again the nature and extent of their involvement should be clearly explained. For most cases, there should not be much of a problem, for example where the specialist is a teacher of the hearing or visually impaired. However, where the specialist is an advisory teacher for emotional and/or behavioural difficulties, or an outreach teacher from any special school or unit, parents need to understand why this person is being asked to look at their child.

Parents unfamiliar with the system for admissions to special schools and units (i.e., usually only after a Statement of special educational needs is finalised) may be alarmed by outreach teachers coming to look at their child. They may fear that the underlying objective is to assess their child for admission to that teacher's own special school or unit. This could lead to them rejecting the involvement of that specialist, or being hostile to any advice given, suspecting a 'hidden agenda'.

Mention of specialist advisory teachers for emotional and behavioural difficulties can strike the same fear into parents' hearts as psychologists. Again, they may fear that their child is being examined because of their 'naughtiness' rather than to help address their difficulties. Parents of children displaying behavioural difficulties are already very vulnerable to criticism of their parenting, and they may see the involvement of this particular specialist as further proof of their inadequacy.

Many of these fears remain unvoiced to members of staff in the school. It is important therefore that SENCOs and other staff be aware of the possibility of these internal reactions in parents, and be ready to address them or prevent them. Clear, concise explanation is essential, preferably both orally and in writing. If the child has been at Stage One or Stage Two, the review meeting will be an ideal opportunity to address these issues, along with the review of progress. If this is not possible, at the very least discussions of this nature should be held in private, and without severe time constraint, to allow parents to discuss the issues that arise.

Where involvement is required from an agency other than the LEA, there may be practical obstacles and protocols that parents find difficult to understand and accept. Specialist medical advice is, technically, confidential. In some cases, the plea of 'confidentiality' can reach ridiculous proportions.

> My child is hearing impaired. The advisory teacher had been involved, but he and the school needed the results of the audiologist's assessment. When approached, the health authority said that medical information was confidential, and would not provide the information. We had to go to our GP for a copy of the audiologist's report, and take a photocopy into school.
>
> (Mrs A, mother of G.)

It is worth investigating the basis on which advice is available from other agencies, and who the operational contacts are likely to be. Very often parents are already working with other professionals, particularly in the medical field, and may be able to offer access to information. However, direct involvement of the medical specialists in school-based assessments is often impracticable. Occupational therapists, physiotherapists and speech and language therapists may all have a role to play in Stage Three assessments, but may be restricted by their own terms and conditions of employment from getting directly involved in new cases in a school.

Even where therapists are coming in to school to see a child, perhaps under the terms of that child's Statement, they will often refuse to see another child in the same school or class, as this contravenes their normal referral procedures. Where a therapist does agree to see another child while on a school visit, they might not be prepared to commit their observations to paper, again because of their own managerial protocols.

This leads to immense frustration on the part of parents as well as schools, who see all advisers as part of their own support team. What starts off as protocol soon becomes seen as obstinacy and 'politics', working against the interests of their child. SENCOs need to develop agreements with the local health authority so that there is a clear referral path, either through the parents or directly through the school nurse or school doctor. It may be that such a framework can only be agreed by senior managers in the education and health authorities. SENCOs should familiarise themselves with local policies and seek to influence change where that is required.

2:101

The Code of Practice states that the SENCO maintains the leading role in the co-ordination of all the various specialists. While this is feasible for external advisers from the local education authority, it is unlikely to be so straightforward in the case of advisers from other agencies. This is where parental involvement can be crucial. Referring back to the discussion in Chapter 3, it can be seen that parents are often the only members of the 'partnership' with direct access to all the professionals who might be involved, or might need to be involved, with their child. The numbers of different medical specialists involved with a child, even before a Statement is produced, can be considerable. Add to that the educational psychologist and all the teachers and there is a considerable team to be fielded and managed. SENCO and parents need to be working together to ensure the most appropriate information and advice is accessed.

At Stage Three, information has to be not only gleaned but also sent out, to the local education authority. Parents should be advised that the local education authority has been notified of their child's Stage Three status, with a clear explanation as to why this has been done.

Deciding whom to involve is a critical element of Stage Three management. The Code of Practice proposes that the SENCO call in an 'appropriate' specialist who is qualified and experienced in the areas of need already identified. This is a cause for concern. It assumes that the SENCO is able to identify and diagnose the child's needs sufficiently clearly to be able to specify which external adviser should be called upon. However, training for SENCOs and other teachers does not include differential diagnosis of, for example, receptive language difficulties, short term auditory memory deficit and behavioural problems. Sometimes it seems to parents that it is a matter of luck whether the right line of investigation is started.

> It was pure chance that my daughter was put into a class where the teacher, new to the school, had experience with remedial teaching. She noticed my daughter had problems with visual input. We referred her to a specialist centre, and it was confirmed that she does not have a 'fixed reference eye'. A year of treatment has not corrected the problem, and nothing more can be done. The present headmaster and his staff are doing all they can to help my daughter. Sadly this was not the case when she started school. She hated it and gradually became school-phobic. She has needed therapy to overcome her fears and it is still ongoing, although she is much improved.
>
> (Mrs W whose daughter has problems with reading and spelling, and low self-confidence.)

For most cases, the answer will be simple: call in the educational psychologist. However, a tremendous assumption is made about the specialist experience and expertise of educational psychologists. It should be remembered that, for the most part, they are generalists. Very few specialise in particular areas of difficulty. Increasingly specialised knowledge is required to differentiate between certain special educational needs, and a generalist psychologist may not always be able to do this. Parents should be consulted about which specialist is to be invited to become involved, as they may themselves have insight into their child's difficulties, through their own research over the period since their child's needs were first identified.

It is important also, at this stage, that parents are given as much information as possible about sources of help for them as parents. Even if a list of voluntary organisations and support groups has already been given to the parents at a previous stage, this should be given again, and if possible, specific groups identified that can provide appropriate information and advice as well as personal support. This is a useful time to provide the parents with a further copy of the school's SEN policy, so that they can be reminded of where Stage Three fits into the overall scheme of support available at the school. If the school has developed a network of parents whose children have special educational needs, renewed contact might be useful at the beginning of Stage Three, so that mutual support of a very local nature can be developed. It is dangerous to assume that, because information was given at a previous stage, the parents will still have access to it, or believe it is still relevant.

Most parents will be fearful for the future. They will be asking themselves, and possibly the school, 'What happens if this fails, too?' It is useful to explain the options at the outset, so that parents will be prepared to face difficult decisions should they be necessary later on. They will be reassured to know that Stage Three is not the 'end of the road' so far as provision and support is concerned, that further intervention is possible through statutory assessment, and possibly Statement, should they be called for. It should be pointed out, of course, that this is not necessarily going to happen.

Some parents will have already undertaken their own investigations of their child's special needs. This might extend to commissioning private advice from chartered psychologists, either educational or clinical, and private tutors. It might include referral through their GP to various specialists, for example, for speech and language or occupational therapy, or multidisciplinary assessments at child development centres. It is important that parents are encouraged to share with the school whatever information they have gathered, as it may shed light on the underlying nature of the difficulty.

Many professionals within the education system are sceptical about the value of independent evidence, particularly from independent private psychologists. However, it should be noted that parents do rely very heavily on the advice they obtain from these sources. It is destructive to the parental partnership to cast serious doubt directly on the advice the parents have gone to great trouble – and sometimes expense – to acquire. Teachers and SENCOs should remain as objective as possible about the information that comes into the assessment process through this route.

In most cases, the findings of the independent specialist will converge with the findings of the LEA specialist, differing often only in the degree of detail contained in the reports. They should be seen as additive and not conflicting in their contribution to the understanding of the child and his or her needs; they can sometimes offer further possible options for provision to meet the needs. They may also shed some light on prognosis, so that realistic targets and objectives can be set.

It is particularly important, in the case of independent psychological advice being sought by parents, that the exact nature of any normative testing used is declared. Many of the tests (such as the Weschler Intelligence Scale for Children and the British Ability Scale) must not be repeated within specific time limits, otherwise the results of both the original and secondary assessment might be invalidated. Whichever testing is done first, the parents must tell the second psychologist about the tests already carried out.

Stage Three: Individual Education Plan

In many respects the structure of the IEP at Stage Three is identical to that at Stage Two, with the specific addition of the involvement of the external specialists. The content, of course, will vary according to the advice received from them. It is very likely that the nature of the needs identified will change according to the observations of these specialists, and that the style and intensity of special provision will be different. It is important that any other advice brought to the school by the parents is also taken into account in writing the IEP.

As with the suggestions for Stage Two, wherever possible, parents should be involved in the development of the IEP, both in respect of assisting the understanding of their child's needs and abilities, and in supporting the provision and monitoring of progress.

The educational psychology assessment

Parents must be advised, preferably in writing, of the date, place and time of the educational psychologist's assessment. Schools should not assume that the psychologist is writing to the parents, nor should the psychologist assume that the school is writing to the parents. SENCOs should work out a general procedure for this so that there is no doubt that the parents are informed. It is a very common complaint by parents that they were not told about the psychologist's appointment, were not invited to attend and were not informed of the outcome of the assessment.

Parents have the right to attend the assessment with their child. Many parents do not, as they recognise that their child may not respond to the psychologist appropriately if their mother or father is also in the room. However, this must be left to the parents' discretion. Any practical difficulties for parents in attending should be discussed directly between the psychologist and the parents.

Even if parents do not attend the assessment itself, there should be sufficient time allocated by the psychologist following the assessment so that the parents can discuss the initial findings face to face. Parents can often shed light on particular aspects of the child's performance in the assessment that can clarify or enhance the test findings. It is also immensely useful to parents to listen to the psychologist's assessment findings, to enhance their own understanding of their child. Although the three stages in the Code of Practice are focused on ensuring that a child can function within the school setting, the parents are concerned for their child's abilities in the wider context – at home, socially, and for the future prospects of employment and independent living. The psychologist's duty is to help all those working with the child to understand the child and to help that child develop and grow. The primary onus on the psychologist is to find ways of helping the child; this will necessarily help the school, but the school is not the 'client'. In the simplest analysis, the child is the client. It is the child whose needs are being assessed, and for whom provision is to be made within school. Parents are, by their relationship to the child, also part of the 'client', as they are the ones with ultimate responsibility for their child's welfare, including his or her education. Although the school is responsible under the Code for identifying and assessing the child's special educational needs, it is merely acting as an agent for the parents in the provision of education.

For this reason, parents should not only be given an opportunity to discuss the findings of the assessment, but should also be sent a copy of any written report following the assessment and discussion. Too often, these reports remain confidential between the psychologist and the school. This is one reason why parents seek independent psychological reports; it is usually not because they do not believe the LEA psychologist's assessment, but because that is the only way for them to access the information. This not only causes unnecessary duplication and expense, but also risks subjecting the child to unnecessary assessments. It is in the child's best interests for the full results of all assessments to be made known to the parents.

Many psychologists believe that parents require more simplified reports than those made available to the schools. This is erroneous. When asked what they perceive to be the benefits of independent psychology reports over LEA psychology reports, the vast majority of parents reply that it is the detail that is most valued. Even if they themselves cannot necessarily understand all the details in a full report – for example, subscale scores – having the information is itself deemed valuable. Where they can, this gives parents a basis for seeking more information to help them understand their child's needs. It also helps them evaluate the provisions that are being made for their child, and understand why some types of provision are more appropriate than others.

After the educational psychologist's report has been circulated, the parents should be given an opportunity to discuss the details further. This may sound very time-consuming, but in fact many parents will not need to do this, particularly if they are being involved at the school in developing and agreeing the individual education plan. However, it provides reassurance to the parents to know that, in principle, they are welcome to contact other members of their child's support team. It is reasonable to offer specific opportunities rather than an 'open door' for such contact, and many psychologists operate a 'clinic' time each week when they will undertake to be available in their office at a certain time on a particular day to take phone calls from parents. Again, in reality, this does not become excessively onerous, but does offer an additional feeling of confidence.

Stage Three: review

2:116

Parents should be invited to attend the Stage Three review. The Code of Practice does not specify who else should be invited to this review, but clearly indicates that the external specialist(s) involved in the assessments and development of the IEP should contribute their opinions on the child's progress.

Parents need to be made aware of the process of review. The date of the review meeting is only part of the review itself. It should be clearly stated what timescale will be covered in the gathering of information on the child's progress and any other assessments that might be made, such as the psychologist's re-evaluation of the child's functioning. This will also give parents time to evaluate their own perceptions of how their child has been coping since the Stage Three IEP has been in place, and what concerns they may still have. It is to be hoped that, wherever possible, more frequent and informal contact will have been made between school and home to keep everyone informed of particular successes or difficulties, and these discussions need to be brought into the context of the more formal review.

The decisions to be made at the review are significant. If the child has made sufficient progress, removal of some support or provision may be suggested; as at Stage Two, this may be viewed with some trepidation by the parents. Again, clarity within the IEP as to which element of special provision was designed to meet which need, together with evidence that that particular need has been overcome or reduced, will be important in providing reassurance to the parents.

Continuation at Stage Three will confirm to the parents that their child does have significant special needs, and they may experience a loss of hope at this point. It is important to keep focusing on the successes within the child's performance, so that parents can maintain a sense of perspective. However, it is again important to confirm to the parents that additional options may be available if further work at Stage Three continues to result in insufficient progress.

If the decision is reached that the child should be referred for statutory assessment, then sufficient time must be allowed in this review meeting for the parents to discuss openly all their concerns about the procedures. It is essential that written information about the process is made available at this time, together with information about parent support groups and voluntary organisations that might be able to offer impartial advice and personal support. As far as possible, the process of referral should be explained, and any forms that the local education authority requires for the referral should be attached to the child's file at the meeting, ready to be filled in later. The timescales involved for the school to complete the referral process should be made clear to the parents. Further contact opportunities should be offered to the parents to discuss the referral once they have absorbed the information they have been given.

Wherever possible, it is helpful to have a space on the referral form for parents to countersign the referral, and to add in any comments they may have regarding their child's special educational needs. Schools should encourage parents to exercise their right to write to the education authority themselves requesting a statutory assessment, and some will be confident enough to do this independently of the school.

3:17 – 3:20

However, some parents may not feel confident, and they might appreciate an opportunity to register in writing their own support for the referral at the time the school makes it. If the parents are actively involved in the referral, this can also obviate the need for them to respond subsequently to the local education authority when they write 'proposing to assess'. Where parents have not asked for a statutory assessment, the local education authority is obliged to give them twenty-nine days to consider whether or not they agree to an assessment. Clearly if all are agreed at the outset, some delay might be avoided. (See next chapter on statutory assessment.)

3:96

There is another reason for suggesting this addition to the school's referral procedures. Parents have the right to appeal to the SEN tribunal if their request for a statutory assessment is turned down by the local education authority. This right of appeal is surrendered if the parents themselves have not written to the local education authority requesting an assessment. It is accepted by the tribunal that where a parent countersigns the school's referral papers, this counts as a direct parental request. Similarly, if the parent has written to the school asking them to refer their child, then this may also count as evidence of a parental request. If the school believes that a statutory assessment is required, after exhausting all their provisions to support a child's special educational needs, then it is only proper that they leave open the possibility of appeal against a decision not to assess.

Other issues at Stage Three

If a child is experiencing general difficulties in school sufficient to warrant a Stage Three intervention, then the difficulties are present on a day-by-day and lesson-by-lesson basis.

It is important that every teacher involved with the child is alert to the full implications of his or her special educational needs, even if they do not directly affect performance in that teacher's particular subject or class. A child having problems in one subject may come to the next period on the timetable in a distressed state. A child with behavioural difficulties may be having problems with classmates, and this can affect how he or she reacts when asked to participate in group work. He or she may suffer from low self-confidence and self-esteem, which can affect general performance even in subjects where no learning difficulty is experienced.

Teachers should be willing to alert the SENCO to incidents they have witnessed around the school involving a child at Stage Three, particularly if it involves bullying or teasing. These children can be very vulnerable.

When speaking with parents informally, perhaps at the end of the school day, teachers need to be honest as well as supportive. Parents do like to hear good news, but do not like to have difficulties brushed aside.

> I did not always feel I was getting the full facts. The teacher said W was accepted – I noted that when she went to sit on the carpet other children blocked the space next to them and said 'You can't sit here, W.' … This year W is more accepted but I note they do not tell me when she is hit or kicked by other children nor recently when she is unkind herself. They did not inform me when she switched off to school two weeks before Christmas – I only discovered this when I mentioned that I had to persuade her to come to school. I feel there is little acknowledgement of her behavioural rather than academic idiosyncrasies.

> (Mrs G, whose daughter W has learning and behavioural problems.)

Parent consultation evenings can be a nightmare for parents of children with significant special educational needs, particularly in secondary school. Going from one subject teacher to another, hearing the same litany of difficulties, can be very demoralising. Often parents give up after seeing a few teachers, or only visit the teachers who will give a reasonably good report. Hopefully these parents are involved in the IEP reviews, and so will have a reasonably clear idea of how their child is getting on. Parent consultation evenings may feel like merely a more public discussion of their child's failings.

Practical points

- *Teachers:* Be aware, when speaking to parents, of their level of understanding of their child's difficulties. They may be feeling very sensitive. Be alert to difficulties in the child during lessons and in less structured times such as playtime and lunch-break. Ensure a clear route of communication with the SENCO.
- *SENCOs:* Ensure maximum involvement of parents in the assessment, planning and review at Stage Three. This will ensure that they are party to successes, and are prepared for further difficult decisions should they be necessary. Ensure all staff who are involved with the child are aware of the nature of the child's difficulties, and understand any particular strategies being used to help the child. Have relevant information available to give to parents.
- *Head teachers:* Ensure that appropriate information is readily available for staff to give to parents, and that appropriate channels of communication with other agencies are known and open.
- *Educational psychologists:* Ensure that parents are advised in advance of the proposed date for your assessments. Find out if any other psychology assessments have been carried out recently. Offer to discuss with parents beforehand the nature of your proposed assessment, and whether or not the parents should attend. Make time available after the assessment to discuss your findings with the parents. Send a copy of your report to the parents. Make time available when you can be contacted by parents to discuss the content of your report.
- *Advisory teachers/outreach teachers:* Explain your role to the parents, or ensure that the SENCO has enough relevant information to explain on your behalf. Ensure that the parents are aware of your involvement *before* you see the child. Copy to the parents any written report or advice.

7 Stage Four – statutory assessment

If an agency such as a Health Authority, or Social Services Department, or a school, considers it necessary to refer a child for a statutory assessment, not only should the parents' views be sought, but also, as discussed in the previous chapter, the parents should be asked to countersign any referral if at all possible.

3:96

This protects the parents' right to appeal to the SEN tribunal should the request for a statutory assessment be turned down.

The decision to refer a child for a statutory assessment is confirmation for parents that their child has very significant difficulties. Any hopes that they could be resolved without further intervention are dashed completely by this decision. While most parents will welcome the fact that additional resources will be used to enable a more thorough assessment of their child's needs, it still remains a bitter blow. Careful and sensitive handling is required for all parents confronted by this decision.

It is also important to stress to parents that the decision to refer will not necessarily result in a statutory assessment. In recent years, the numbers of children being referred, particularly among those already attending school, has escalated far beyond the anticipated levels. Local education authorities plan for so many assessments per year; estimates of the cost of statutory assessments range from £3,000 to £10,000. Education authorities do not commit that level of funds lightly. If the child is at school, there should be an agreement between the school and parents as to what will be done for the child pending the outcome of an assessment, or in the event of an assessment being refused.

Timescales

3:27 – 3:30

Since the implementation of the 1993 Education Act, the statutory assessment process is regulated in terms of timescales. There are four distinct phases in the process. (See Table 7.1 on p.108 for a summary.)

A: Weeks one to six: process of information-gathering to decide whether or not a statutory assessment is required.

B: Weeks seven to sixteen: the 'assessment' period of gathering evidence and advice to decide whether or not to issue a Statement. Full advice from each adviser is supposed to be submitted within the first six weeks of this period.

C: Weeks seventeen and eighteen: drafting of proposed Statement or Note in Lieu.

D: Weeks nineteen to twenty-six: period allowed to finalise Statement.

Time saved in one phase cannot accrue to the next phase. Thus if the local education authority takes only two weeks to decide to proceed with an assessment, they cannot then take fourteen weeks for the assessment period.

During phase A, schools and educational psychologists should be ready to offer any advice or evidence requested by the education authority within the given timescales. Failure to do so may result in a request for an assessment being turned down, on the grounds that sufficient evidence was not forthcoming.

3:40

The only exceptions to the six-week time limit for phase A are:

- where advice is sought from the child's school around the time of a school holiday lasting four weeks or more
- where there are exceptional personal circumstances affecting the child or his or her parents
- where the child or parents are absent for a period of four weeks or more.

Therefore, if it is only pressure of work that causes a school or psychologist to delay their response, the result is likely to be a rejection of the referral, rather than a delay to the decision. This is against the child's interests. Schools and educational psychologists should be able to respond to any request for further information regarding the referral to enable the local education authority to decide within six weeks whether or not to proceed with an assessment.

3:41

There are exceptions to the time limits for phase B. In addition to those for phase A, these are:

- where the local education authority seeks additional advice from the school, psychologist or other agency subsequent to receiving their initial full advice
- where the parents have asked to provide additional advice after the initial six-week period
- where the health or social services authorities have not replied within six weeks

- where the child fails to attend an appointment for an assessment.

One of the most common causes of delay is found in the health service, where there can be difficulties co-ordinating input from the many different medical specialists who may be involved with the child. It is important, therefore, that parents are encouraged to identify at the outset the different specialists whose opinion may be valuable in the assessment; they should then notify the Named Officer at the education authority and the designated medical officer. These officers can then arrange for the reports to be requested. Additionally, if the child is due to see one of their specialists within the coming few months, perhaps for a regular annual check-up, the parents can be encouraged to ask for an earlier appointment, and advise their specialist that the child is undergoing a statutory assessment. The consultation can then be geared to providing an appropriate report within the prescribed timescales.

It is equally important for parents to seek to agree appointment times that can be honoured. Parents may wish to contact the designated medical officer at the outset to arrange the medical appointments, so they can avoid being offered an appointment that cannot be met.

There are no exceptions to the two-week time limit for phase C.

3:43

There are exceptions to the eight-week time limit for phase D:

- if the parents are absent for four weeks or more, or there are other exceptional family circumstances that prevent parents responding in the given time
- if the parents want to take longer than the given fifteen days to make representations about the proposed Statement, or require more than one meeting to discuss the proposed Statement
- where the Secretary of State takes longer than two weeks to give consent to the child being placed in a non-approved school.

Sections 165 and 167 of the 1993 Education Act indicate that local education authorities are required to make a statutory assessment of a child for whom they are responsible who has special educational needs and who probably needs a Statement. This means that it should be likely that the assessment process will result in a Statement. However, it does not mean that it is inevitable. The assessment is in itself a process of 'finding out', of diagnosis. It should not be seen merely as a Statementing process. That term really only applies to the last ten weeks of the twenty-six weeks shown in the timetable: that is, two weeks to draft a Statement and eight more weeks to finalise it.

The local education authority may issue a 'Note in Lieu' of a Statement (see later in this chapter). This is issued when, after gathering all the evidence, it is decided that the child can be supported from resources available to his or her school, without additional intervention from LEA resources. This in itself is proof that the statutory assessment is a diagnostic process, and not merely the means of determining a Statement.

By the same token, the criteria for deciding whether or not a statutory assessment is required must be different from the criteria for deciding whether or not a Statement is required. These are two separate decisions, based on two quite different sets of evidence, and take place approximately ten weeks apart.

Criteria for statutory assessment

3:46 – 3:94

The Code of Practice gives quite considerable guidance as to the sort of evidence that is required to support a request for a statutory assessment. Most LEAs, however, will have produced their own versions of these criteria, which more closely reflect local allocation of resources to schools under Local Management of Schools (LMS), and local decision-making processes. However, the local criteria should not differ in intention from those laid out in the Code of Practice.

One area in the Code's criteria that is unclear is that concerning children who have more than one special educational need, but of whom no individual category of need is sufficiently significant to warrant statutory assessment. Increasingly, children are being identified who may have a mixture of difficulties, perhaps relating to reading, spelling, receptive language and motor co-ordination. The interaction of the difficulties leads to a complex picture of a child who is not achieving, and whose combined special educational needs lead to a likely need for intervention beyond the resources of the school. In such cases, those making the referral must ensure that evidence of the combined difficulties is presented sufficiently clearly to support a decision to assess. Indeed, the way evidence is presented at initial referral is crucial to the decision-making process. It should not be assumed by parents or any other professional that the officers understand the full implications of the 'diagnosis' or label with which the child initially presents.

> When I requested a formal assessment, I was told that 'the school would be able to meet H's needs from their existing resources,' which I totally disagreed with. If I had not kicked up a fuss I would not have got H Statemented. My impression is that they have pigeon holes for stereotyped children, i.e. Down's syndrome, dyslexia etc. The officer agreed with me that she had no knowledge

of congenital muscular dystrophy and it wasn't until she saw H that she realised she would miss out without being Statemented.

(Mrs A, who worked for a year to persuade the local education authority to conduct a statutory assessment.)

The criteria for assessment clearly demonstrate the benefit of well-defined individual education plans at Stage Two and/or Stage Three for children already at school. The types of evidence regarding the special needs, the depth of detail about the provisions already made, and the recorded advice and input of external specialists, all contribute to make a case for more intensive and/or extensive intervention, likely to require additional resources from the local education authority.

It is important that parents are made aware of the criteria for assessment so that they can also decide what kind of evidence they might wish to provide; this might include gathering further evidence in support of the referral from other specialists not directly involved with the school.

The parental contribution

3:100

The Code of Practice gives some guidance for parents writing their own contribution. Appendix B expands on this.

It should be remembered that, for most parents, writing a report about their child is both difficult and painful. Many parents will not be experienced in writing reports at all, and even those who are, from their own professional experience, may be ill-equipped for the challenge of writing about someone so close to them.

I had put off and put off writing the report on W. When I sat down to do it I finally finished at 1.30 in the morning it was due in. I have done CVs and forms for many people so I was astonished at how difficult I found it to be articulate when writing on an emotive subject.

(Mrs G, whose own background includes teaching and personnel.)

Most people only write about members of their family in informal communications, perhaps in letters or in Christmas cards. When they do write, it is nearly always about the positive things, the achievements, the progress and the developments. Even when writing to someone who knows the family well, they are unlikely to make more than a passing mention of the difficulties or problems faced by a family with a special needs child.

Writing in a critical way, examining all the limitations or difficulties in a child, can be very distressing emotionally for a parent. Some parents have described it as a feeling of betrayal, to write so critically of their own child. These feelings are heightened by the fact that they are writing this report for a total stranger, someone who may share the information with other strangers, who will be making judgements and decisions based on the information given.

Professionals supporting parents through this stage of assessment need to bear this emotional reaction in mind and help the parents overcome their feelings to make their own report. If parents still feel they cannot write a report, they should be offered help, perhaps having someone else write down what they want to say.

Writing parental contributions

Most psychologists and many schools will record parental views in some way on their own submissions, but these tend to be very brief, such as 'parents wish their son to be educated in mainstream', or 'parents are happy with their daughter's current placement'. This does not constitute parental contribution.

When a professional does offer to act as scribe for parents, a specific appointment should be made for them to do this, rather than combining it with an assessment or review meeting. It is essential that professionals do not 'filter' what parents say when writing down their contributions for them. Parents may need help to go into detail about examples of their child's behaviour, achievements and difficulties, and they should be encouraged to talk about their child's successes as well as limitations. The guidance notes at Appendix B can be used as an interview guide so that all the relevant information is included.

Further parental involvement

Parents have an important role to play in the management of their own child's 'case' through the assessment process. There is an active role for them in liaising with professionals and progressing the information through the system. They can sometimes put pressure on people to submit reports more quickly, whereas the local education authority may be bound by protocol when chasing late submissions. They should at the very least be encouraged to keep note of the dates when each phase of the assessment process is due to finish, so that they can check when decisions are being made.

Barriers to parental involvement

2:28

The Code of Practice emphasises the importance of parental involvement in the identification and assessment of their child's special needs, and makes the point that the absence of parental involvement diminishes the effectiveness of the professionals' help. Too many assessments proceed without meaningful contributions from parents. This section looks at why parents sometimes fail to get involved, and looks at some of the ways that this can be overcome.

Emotions

Chapter 1 examined how parents react to the fact of their child having special needs. It is clear that they experience a tremendous and traumatic rotation of emotions. These emotions are present whether the child has severe, profound difficulties, or relatively non-disabling difficulties. The intensity of the feelings is not directly proportional to the severity of the disability; and the feelings do not go away. The process of assessment can often rekindle many of the negative feelings of guilt, hopelessness and resentment, as well as anger and frustration, that may be suppressed while the parents cope with day-to-day life. Formal assessment re-examines many of the early phases of realisation, diagnosis and setbacks that parents may have thought they had left behind. It comes as a great shock to them when they again experience a resurgence of feelings that may have lain dormant for several years. In parents for whom the formal assessment is the first real opportunity to look at the totality of their child's difficulties, all the emotions of diagnosis and realisation are, of course, being experienced for the first time.

It is not pleasant.

Parents may be afraid of having to experience those feelings again. They have buried them as deeply as they can over the years, while getting on with their everyday lives, and resurrecting all the hurt and pain is not an option that they actively seek out. They may also perceive that their feelings are a barrier to having their views taken seriously, that the professionals will in some way mistrust their judgement because of the strong overlay of emotion.

Trust

Parents often feel they cannot trust the professionals with whom they deal during the assessment. Many parents whose children have had their special needs identified for some time may have experienced a breach of trust somewhere along the way, although not necessarily within the education system. Some will have felt let down by medical personnel, perhaps through delays with referrals or mishandling of disclosure or diagnosis in the early stages. They may have been dealt with insensitively by social workers or other people in authority, including negative experiences of claiming benefits or getting help with housing. For many parents, the boundaries between one agency and another become blurred, and the fact that these 'new' professionals are from the education department will make no difference. Trust is a very easy thing to break, and a very difficult thing to repair.

Even their experience of helpful professionals may prove counter-productive in the development of trust. Teachers and others who offer a sympathetic ear but who do not deliver what appears to have been promised are bundled into the same category as the Benefits Agency office that appears to withhold deliberately information on available grants and allowances.

Mistrust leads to suspicion, which in turn can lead to further mistrust. Parents often feel that there is a collaboration, or conspiracy, among the professionals, to exclude them from the assessment process. It is clear to them that the professionals talk to one another about their decisions and ideas, but rarely include the parents or let them know what discussions have taken place. Part of this suspicion arises from the long periods of time that elapse during the formal assessment process. Even within the timescale of twenty-six weeks, the 'gathering evidence' period of only ten weeks is the equivalent of a term. For a pre-school child, this can represent a considerable proportion of his or her entire life; for a child at school, it is a third of the school year. Parents believe that *something* must be going on during that time; the fact that no one is talking to them about it therefore must mean that decisions are being made behind their backs. This sounds like sheer paranoia, but in fact is a commonly encountered belief, and a real fear.

Formality

The statutory assessment is often known as a 'formal assessment', and many of the meetings that parents attend during the process are indeed very formal; at least they feel formal to the parents. They may be very nervous at meeting with some of the specialists whom they may be seeing for the first time. Even those specialists who are known to them may still be held in such high regard – because of their position and the amount of power they are perceived to wield – that parents do not make best use of the opportunities to discuss the professional's findings, or their own views.

The procedures themselves are formal procedures. Parents are usually encountering them for the first time. They lack experience, and lack confidence in the outcome. Officers, psychologists, SENCOs and head teachers have all had more experience than the parents in going through the assessment. For the parents, it is their child's future that is at stake; they cannot afford to make any mistakes. Yet the complexity of it all seems purpose-designed to allow mistakes to happen. Parents generally do not have colleagues or manuals to tell them how the system works. 'Trial and error' is a frightening concept. They are at the mercy of the system, and, more to the point, at the mercy of the individuals within the system responsible for progressing their child's interests.

Parents' own special needs

Many children with special needs have parents with special needs. Some of the difficulties that are encountered are familial: for example, dyslexia, some language disorders, some types of general learning difficulties, and some forms of sensory impairment. The parents themselves therefore may have difficulty either understanding the procedures that are being undertaken, or expressing their own views either in writing or orally. For parents of a different cultural or linguistic background, there is the added difficulty of interpretation or translation, and the problems of explaining their own cultural priorities for their child alongside their views on the child's special needs.

In addition, the adult population suffers from the same random difficulties that affect our children. Sensory, language, and learning difficulties can affect any parent of any child. These parents may feel unwilling to expose their own inadequacies through trying to write or speak about their child's difficulties.

Lack of confidence

This is not so much lack of confidence in the system or the professionals, but lack of confidence in the parents' own knowledge, in the relevance of their own experience.

> When they asked for my views on G's special educational needs, I thought, 'I don't know about education, so I can't really say.' Then the befriender reminded me that I *do* know G: how she is, what she is like, what she can and can't do. I realised that I am an expert, an expert in my own child. That helped me get down to writing about G and what help she needed.
>
> (Mr H, whose daughter G is profoundly deaf.)

This attitude can lead to parental belief that they should just 'leave it the experts'. By so doing, they deprive their child of the benefit of their input, and may also find themselves in later conflict with the authority when they read the professionals' reports and disagree with some of the key findings. At that stage, the discussions are carried out more in anger and frustration, on both sides, when a positive and thoughtful contribution in the early stages of the assessment might have enabled the 'experts' to understand the child better, and interpret their own findings differently.

Access to and use of independent evidence

Children who have a range of difficulties, or difficulties with a range of implications, may have been seen over the years by a host of different 'experts'. Parents often do not realise that the information contained in some of these early reports may offer an insight into aspects of their child's current and future needs. They can be used in several ways. They can act as a prompt to the parents when writing about their child's developmental history, so that they can remind themselves of previous difficulties that have been overcome; they can remind parents of the onset of difficulties and the impact they had on the child's ability to function. They can be submitted as specialist evidence to support a parent's understanding of their child's needs, condition or disability. They can often act as signposts for further investigations that may need to be carried out during the formal assessment. Findings by a paediatrician or clinical psychologist in previous years, for example, may have indicated that the child may suffer from a language disorder; this may not have been followed up at the time for a variety of reasons, but might indicate that a speech and language assessment during Stage Four could be useful.

Desire to prove the LEA wrong

Some parents deliberately withhold their own knowledge, including that of independent specialists who have provided reports, as a sort of test for the authority, to see 'whether they are clever enough to work it out for themselves'. They fear that, by disclosing their own expert evidence too soon, they will give the authority time to find reasons to argue with the independent advice. This attitude is largely borne out of mistrust, and may be exacerbated by a desire to play a trump at the final hand. Needless to say it is unconstructive, but reflects a real perception on the part of parents that control over their own child's life is being taken away from them, and that, by holding on to their evidence until the last minute, they can regain that control over the process. There is an element of competitiveness about this approach, where the parents believe, for example, that their

)gist knows more about their child's syndrome than the LEA who can therefore be discredited. These are often the join the process as if it were a battle, and for whom the process or conflict becomes more important than the outcome for their child. This is not to be condemned; it is a strategy frequently born of bitter experience with other agencies and experts, and employed as a means of self defence.

Overcoming the barriers to participation

So, given these various obstacles, how can professionals help to overcome them, and assist parents to participate fully in the process?

Firstly, providing parents with information is the key. This should include:

- the timetable for the process
- who is involved: each individual professional; what their role is; what they will do; why they should be involved
- the assessments the child will need to undergo during the Stage Four process: the educational psychology assessment, the medical, and any other specifically arranged assessments
- the range of additional specialists who may be asked for their advice: this must be done in consultation with the parents, so that any further specialists can be added to the fact-finding process
- the name of the officer who can be contacted for further information, and how they can be contacted, for example if there are specific times when they are available
- what provision (if any) will be made for the child while the assessment is taking place
- what decisions the parents will be asked to make at the various points in the process
- what the parents' rights are: of involvement; of appeal if they are not satisfied with the outcome
- how to go about making their own contribution to the assessment
- how their child's own views might be taken into account
- where the parents can go for further help and support, including a list of voluntary organisations and parent support groups
- schools available in the area, highlighting any which might be deemed particularly appropriate (although not prejudging the outcome of the assessment)
- if there is a parent partnership scheme in operation, who to contact to find out more.

Any communication with parents during the assessment process must be given clearly, preferably in person and in writing, with sufficient opportunity for the parents to take in the information and ask questions to clarify. Standard letters used by the local education authority should be checked for ease of understanding and ease of reading. The style of these letters is important, too. Cold third-person tones do little to encourage parents to trust the author. For example, wherever possible, the letter should replace references to 'the LEA will do such and such' with 'I will do such and such'. The LEA officer signing the letter is acting on behalf of the education authority, and so takes on the corporate responsibility in carrying out their role. Writing in the first person just makes it more 'user-friendly'.

Where there are active parent partnership links between the local education authority and the voluntary sector, it may be useful to ask parent representatives from the voluntary groups to check through the standard letters being used. They are more familiar with how these letters are received, and can give helpful suggestions for improvements that change the style without compromising the content. A similar consultation is useful when local education authorities are drafting information leaflets for parents, for example about the process of the assessment, or the role of the educational psychologist.

The information needs to be accessible, and capable of being readily assimilated. All too often, the provision of 'information' at the beginning of the assessment process consists of a large collection of leaflets, brochures and other pieces of paper that arrive together with the formal notice of assessment. Parents may not be able to weed out the specific elements that apply to them, and they may never actually read the leaflets at all unless directed to the most relevant parts. In particular, it may be helpful to ensure that the parents' first language is the one used in any written materials sent regarding the assessment. This includes the use of tape-recorded information for parents with visual impairment or poor literacy skills, and of course Braille for readers of Braille. The RNIB can advise how to commission translation of leaflets and other documents into Braille (see Appendix C). Professionals already involved with the family, such as advisory teachers, SENCOs or educational psychologists, may be useful sources of information regarding the most appropriate form of language.

3.14

Parents will also welcome personal contact with key individuals during the process. The Code of Practice suggests that the letter informing the parents of a proposal to assess may be delivered personally. However, pressure of time means that this one-to-one support by various professionals may not always be available or practicable.

SENCOs could play an important role for parents of children already at school who are referred for Stage Four assessments. They can encourage the parents to make an appointment when the notice to assess first arrives, and offer to go through the information with them, making practical suggestions as to how the parents can best participate in their child's assessment. Similarly, advisory teachers, or Portage workers for those with severe learning difficulties, may be able to fulfil this role for pre-school children. If available, education welfare officers may be able to do this.

One possible approach is to offer 'seminars' to parents whose children are just beginning Stage Four assessments, where they can meet for mutual support, and have the information provided not only in written or taped forms, but also face to face, so that questions can be asked and answered, and the most relevant parts of the information can be highlighted. During the course of any one term a single Named Officer is likely to have a number of children beginning the assessment process, and arranging meetings on a group basis would certainly be less time-consuming than seeing each parent or set of parents individually. This might be an opportunity to 'match' Named Persons to families who seem to be in greatest need of support, so that misunderstanding and conflict can be prevented later on in the process. Individual follow-up can be arranged for parents who are identified as needing additional help.

Where active parent partnership schemes are in place, either through the local education authority or through the voluntary sector, a positive approach would involve that scheme in the provision of advisers for such seminars, so that parents have an opportunity to meet with other parents who have been through the process, rather than just with the officers or other professionals of the authority.

Discussions in meetings can often be hurried, owing to time pressures for both professionals and parents. This can give the impression that the professional is not interested in helping the parents understand the new advice, or the implications of proposals about provision. This can add to the mistrust or suspicion that the parents may already be feeling, and serves only to widen the perceived gulf between their own viewpoint and that of 'the authority'. This feeling of conflict or confrontation can exist even where there is no actual disagreement between the parents and the professionals about the child's needs and the provision required to meet the needs. It can encourage the parents to seek out points of disagreement, believing that they must have an opposing view in order to be 'fighting' for their child's educational rights.

Good open contact with key professionals will help allay mistrust, and should serve to prevent a confrontational approach by parents.

What parents want most of all is honesty. They know that no single 'expert' will necessarily have all the answers. When teachers, or psychologists, or officers, pretend that they do, the parents become sceptical and may mistrust the advice they receive. It is perfectly acceptable for parents to be told 'I don't know', or 'I'm not sure', even about things that professionals feel they should know or be sure about. Where there are other sources of information that can provide the answers, these should be offered to the parents directly, or an offer made to find out more on their behalf. It remains true, however, that where there is no answer, or no absolute answer, parents would rather hear this than be fobbed off with a half-truth or statement of wishful thinking.

Advice

In addition to asking the parents for their contribution, the local education authority will seek the following advice:

- educational advice, from the child's school, or from an advisory teacher if the child is not at school
- psychological advice, from the educational psychologist employed by or contracted to the local education authority
- medical advice, from the designated medical officer, who is empowered to gather other medical advice from any health authority involved with the child
- social services report, if the child is already known to the social services department.

It is important for each professional to be aware of the other elements in the assessment. Parents, too, need to know that each of the above elements are gathered separately; the fact that the school has submitted its report does not imply that the evidence of the medical officer or psychologist has also been submitted. Parents often believe that the school, or the psychologist, gathers the various pieces of advice together and then submits them to the education authority; careful explanation can avoid this misunderstanding.

The psychologist may need to conduct an additional assessment, even though one may have been done during a recent Stage Three review. As with a Stage Three assessment, the parents must be notified of the appointment in advance, and given the opportunity to meet the psychologist to discuss the findings. If possible, the psychologist should send a copy of their report to the parents at the same time one is sent to the local education authority, so that parents have an opportunity to discuss the contents with the psychologist before any statement is drafted.

This can save time and aggravation in the later phases.

> The educational psychologist misunderstood my child's problems and therefore her report was not accurate. She did not show me this report before sending it off and therefore my draft statement reflected her incorrect understanding. A lot of time was wasted and four draft statements issued. This could have been avoided if information had been discussed and shared at the start.

> (Mrs Q, whose daughter has speech and language difficulties.)

If the parents have provided independent psychological advice, there may be a need to compare this with the LEA psychological advice. Although in many instances the independent advice will concur with the LEA advice, there are occasions when disputes arise. Parents are willing to accept a decision based on reasoned argument, but will not be content if the education authority merely prefers its own advice automatically.

> The local education authority EP had been working on a verbal IQ, rather than the non-verbal. He had blocked all requests by me and the head teacher for extra help, believing the lack of speech was due to a low IQ. He insisted my son should transfer from lower school to the MLD school at age nine.
> The independent psychologist gave a far higher IQ and advised specialist speech and language school. The local education authority EP reviewed his findings and then apologised, as he now got the same results.
> My son went to a speech and language school at twelve years seven months. The local education authority EP maintained to the end that an MLD school would meet my son's needs, even knowing the head of the MLD school had told me my son needed a speech and language school.

> (Mrs Q, whose son has high-level language disorder.)

If there is a dispute between two sets of advice, the local education authority must indicate why it has preferred one piece of advice over another.

Educational advice should also be shared with the parents before it is submitted, so that any misunderstandings can be handled quickly and face to face.

Medical advice often causes difficulties, as the role of the designated medical officer is not always understood either by LEA officers, or by the health authority. If clear procedures and responsibilities have not been set out, the result can be an uncoordinated response to the education authority's request for medical advice.

> The DMO examined my son at the EBD school. Her report was three lines in length and she had not looked at any of the other reports, e.g. from the London teaching hospital, speech therapy, etc. I had to write to my son's paediatrician before anything was done. I found out that the DMO had left it to the

headmaster of the EBD school to decide if my son needed occupational therapy. He was therefore denied this therapy for a further two years, even though it was available from the local hospital.

(Mrs S, whose son Q has Asperger syndrome with language and motor co-ordination difficulties.)

If parents have sight of reports before they are submitted, they can help to ensure that all the relevant information is included, and that any factual inaccuracies are corrected before the statement is drafted.

Much of the content of the educational psychologist and head teacher's report was not discussed with me. Some of the remarks were insensitive and totally untrue. I did have a further opportunity, after the draft statement was issued, to discuss the content with the head teacher, and some of the remarks have since been withdrawn. Some information which was vital to include had been omitted when the reports were sent to the local education authority.

(Mrs A, whose son has language difficulties and associated behavioural and learning difficulties.)

There is no issue of confidentiality, as all the reports submitted during the assessment will be made available subsequently for parents to see, as appendices either to the draft statement or to the Note in Lieu.

The child's own views

3:120

Since the advent of the Children Act, it has become widely recognised that children have a right to express their views on how they are treated and dealt with. This extends to the assessment of special educational needs. The Code of Practice gives some guidance on the issue.

Parents may feel that they want to be involved in helping their child express and record his or her own views. Sometimes they may try to influence what their child says, and may 'filter' what is written down. Parents should be encouraged to acknowledge that their child has his or her own views, and that these have a right to be heard separately from their own.

It may be appropriate for a teacher, psychologist or other professional to act as the facilitator in recording the child's views, and again care must be taken not to edit what is said and written, or to influence unduly what the child says.

Some children may not be able to express their thoughts, through either lack of literacy, lack of language or some other inhibitory factor. Close attention should be paid in these circumstances to non-verbal reactions from the child to different situations that might reflect the various future options for the child.

Wherever possible, the child's own views should be recorded within the assessment separately from those of all other contributors.

The role of the Named Person

Where an appropriate scheme is operational, it is helpful to explain to parents the benefit of having a Named Person. In the initial stages of the implementation of the Code of Practice, many parents have indicated that they do not want this sort of help. This may be because they are unaware of the benefits, or unaware of the difficulties of coping with the statutory assessment process.

3:102

The Code of Practice encourages local education authorities to promote the idea of the Named Person to parents at the time they are asked to make their own contribution to the assessment. Other professionals should also support this, as it will reduce the parents' reliance on SENCOs, teachers and psychologists, reducing their time involvement to more manageable proportions.

Note in Lieu of a statement

4:17 – 4:22

After gathering all the evidence, the local education authority will decide whether or not to issue a proposed Statement of special educational needs.

The agreement to proceed with a statutory assessment does not necessarily guarantee that a Statement will be forthcoming. The local education authority may decide, after gathering all the evidence, that the child's needs can be met from resources already available to the school he or she currently attends.

In this case, the authority is encouraged to issue a Note in Lieu of a Statement, that pulls together all the evidence and advice gathered during the assessment, and may identify the child's needs and appropriate provision in the same format as a Statement.

In the case of a Note in Lieu, however, the local education authority bears no responsibility for ensuring any implementation of the provision specified. Schools should look on a Note in Lieu as an important piece of advice that can inform their development of an individual education plan for the child, who reasonably should be maintained at Stage Three for at least a term. Following implementation of the advice contained in the Note, the school may subsequently refer the child for another assessment. If the parents wish to request another assessment, they must wait at least six months after the previous assessment was carried out.

If the education authority has decided not to issue a Statement, the parents can appeal to the SEN tribunal (see Chapter 10).

Practical points

- *Teachers:* Be clear about the procedures that will be followed during the assessment. Particularly in primary schools, parents may seek information via their child's class teacher about how the assessment is progressing. If asked to help record the child's own views or the parents' contribution, be prepared to provide a full and honest account of their views.
- *SENCOs:* Be clear about the procedures, and who the key personnel are at the local education authority and other agencies. Assist the parents in making appropriate appointments for medicals and psychologists' assessments. Be clear with the parents about what support will be given to their child pending the outcome of the assessment. If asked to help record the child's own views or the parents' contribution, be prepared to provide a full and honest account of their views.
- *Head teachers:* Ensure that the school has procedures in place for providing prompt replies to requests for additional information during the assessment process. Make sure copies of reports submitted during the assessment are made available to parents at the same time. Be prepared to offer a meeting to discuss the content of your report with the parents.
- *School governors:* Ensure that your school has sufficient resources in staff time and information packs to support parents whose children are undergoing assessment.
- *Educational psychologists:* Offer time to parents before and after any assessments to answer questions and listen to their views. If asked to help record the child's own views or the parents' contribution, be prepared to provide a full and honest account of their views. Write reports promptly and send copies to parents at the same time they are submitted to the local education authority.
- *DMOs:* Clarify your role, and the protocols within your health authority for gathering information from a variety of specialists. Be prepared to

chase these additional reports if they are not forthcoming. Clarify your role with the education authority, so that everyone is confident about who is doing what.

- *Named Officers*: Be clear in requests for information. Offer parents access to support so that they can maximise their involvement. Keep parents informed about any delays in the process, and the reasons for them.
- *Parent Partnership Officers*: Seek opportunities to help parents individually or in groups so that they understand the process. Identify members of the voluntary sector who might be able to offer assistance.

Table 7.1 Statementing timetable

	Each phase	Running total
LEA receives request for statutory assessment		
A: LEA decides whether or not to assess	Six weeks	Six weeks
B: LEA seeks and receives advice LEA decides whether or not to issue Statement	(Six weeks) Ten weeks	Sixteen weeks
C: LEA issues draft statement or notice (possibly as Note in Lieu)	Two weeks	Eighteen weeks
D: LEA finalises Statement	Eight weeks	Twenty-six weeks

8 The Statement

4:37

The first document that is produced once the local education authority has decided that it is necessary to issue a Statement of special educational needs is the 'proposed Statement' or draft Statement. This is the authority's suggested wording for the summarisation of the needs, objectives, and desired provision for the child, based solely on the information provided during the assessment by the various professionals and the parents, including where possible the child's own views. This document should be produced within two weeks of the local education authority receiving all the evidence, representations and advice gathered during the assessment process; that is, no more than eighteen weeks after the authority first received a referral for the statutory assessment, or twelve weeks after the authority first notified the parents that it had decided to conduct a statutory assessment.

3:36

For parents, this will have been an anxious time, and the apparent deathly silence that descends on the process towards the end can be almost unbearable. If the child is at school, the SENCO should be prepared to support parents through this period; for pre-school children this might require the involvement of the advisory teacher, psychologist or Portage worker. Parents fear the worst; they know that the Statement is an important document, and anticipation of its arrival can be very stressful. Parents should be encouraged to identify the date when they can expect to receive the proposed Statement, and resist the temptation to undertake too many 'chasing' phone calls before then.

However, if this date passes with no sign of the proposed Statement, parents should be encouraged to contact the Named Officer to identify the cause of the delay, and agree another date by which the proposed Statement may be delivered. The Code of Practice does not specify any exceptions to the two weeks' time limit for producing the proposed Statement, so excessive delay would be a suitable cause for complaint. SENCOs, advisory teachers and others supporting the parents should be prepared to help them make the appropriate complaint as necessary.

4:38

In addition to the parents, each of those who gave advice during the

110

assessment stage should also receive a copy of the proposed Statement. In the case of medical advice, the proposed Statement is likely to be sent only to the designated medical officer, rather than to all the individual therapists and specialists who might have provided some information. Similarly professionals who have provided evidence for the parents to submit will not be sent a copy of the proposed Statement. It is left to the discretion of the designated medical officer, and the parents, to circulate the information more widely. Although the Code of Practice and Regulations do not indicate whether anyone other than the parents can make representations about the proposed Statement, any professional who has submitted advice should read the statement carefully, together with the appendices, to ensure that no misrepresentations of their own advice have occurred. Where professionals feel that there is a disparity between the advice given and its representation in the proposed statement, parents should be advised of this so that they can judge whether they wish to take the matter further. Parents often come to rely on the experts and specialists who assess their child, and it would be a breach of their trust for a professional to see an error and take no action.

Parents have only fifteen days to lodge any disagreement with the content of the Statement, although there is the opportunity of a full eight weeks to agree any changes.

Figure 8.1

Statement format

Part 1: Introduction

1. In accordance with section 168 of the Education Act 1993 ('the Act') and the Education (Special Educational Needs) Regulations 1994 ('the Regulations'), the following Statement is made by [*the name of the education authority*] ('the authority') in respect of the child whose name and other particulars are mentioned below.

Child

Surname........................... Other names.....................
Home address..................... ....
....
.... Sex................................
.... Religion..........................
Date of Birth..................... Home language ....

Child's parent or person responsible

Surname........................... Other names.....................
Home address..................... ....
.... Relationship to child ....
....
Telephone number ....

Figure 8.1 continued

2. When assessing the child's special educational needs the authority took into consideration, in accordance with regulation 10 of the Regulations, the representations, evidence and advice set out in the Appendices to this Statement.

Part 2: Special educational needs

[Here will be set out the child's special educational needs, in terms of the child's learning difficulties which call for special educational provision, as assessed by the authority. Each of the child's SENs must be identified.]

Part 3: Special educational provision

Objectives
[Here will be specified the objectives which the special educational provision for the child should aim to meet.]

Educational provision to meet needs and objectives
[Here will be specified the special educational provision which the authority consider appropriate to meet the needs specified in Part 2 and to meet the objectives specified above, and which in particular should specify –

(a) any appropriate facilities and equipment, staffing arrangements and curriculum,
(b) any appropriate modifications to the National Curriculum,
(c) any appropriate exclusions from the application of the National Curriculum, in detail, and the provision which it is proposed to substitute for any such exclusions in order to maintain a balanced and broadly-based curriculum; and
(d) where residential accommodation is appropriate, that fact.]

Monitoring
[Here will be specified the arrangement to be made for –

(a) regularly monitoring progress in meeting the objectives specified in this Part,
(b) establishing targets in furtherance of those objectives,
(c) regularly monitoring the targets referred to in (b),
(d) regularly monitoring the appropriateness of any modifications to the application of the National Curriculum, and
(e) regularly monitoring the appropriateness of any provision substituted for exclusions from the application of the National Curriculum.

Here also will be specified any special arrangements for reviewing this Statement.]

Part 4: Placement

[Here will be specified – in the final statement, but not the proposed Statement –

(a) the type of school which the authority consider appropriate for the child and the name of the school for which the parents has expressed a preference or, where the authority are required to specify the name of a school, the name of the school which they consider would be appropriate for the child and should be specified, or
(b) the provision for his/her education otherwise than at a school which the authority consider appropriate.]

112

Figure 8.1 continued

Part 5: Non-educational needs

[Here will be specified the non-educational needs of the child for which the authority consider provision is appropriate if the child is to benefit properly from the special educational provision specified in Part 3.]

Part 6: Non-educational provision

[Here will be specified any non-educational provision which the authority propose to make available or which they are satisfied will be made available by a district health authority, a social services authority or some other body, including the arrangements for its provision. Also specified will be the objectives of the provision and the arrangements for monitoring the progress in meeting those objectives.]

....

Date   A duly authorised officer of the authority

Appendices

Appendix A: Parental representations
[Any written representations made by the parent(s) regarding the LEA's proposal to assess, and a summary which the parent has accepted as accurate of any oral representations so made, or a record that no representations were made.]

Appendix B: Parental evidence
[Any written evidence submitted by the parent or a record that no such evidence was submitted.]

Appendix C: Advice from the child's parent
[Any written advice from the parent submitted during the assessment process, including any written record of parental advice given verbally, which the parent has agreed is an accurate record.]

Appendix D: Educational advice
[Advice submitted by the child's school, or if not at school, an advisory teacher.]

Appendix E: Medical advice
[Advice submitted by the designated medical officer including any specialist advice provided by other therapists or specialists within the Health Authority or known to be involved with the child.]

Appendix F: Psychological advice
[Advice submitted by the LEA educational psychologist.]

Appendix G: Advice from the social services authority
[If the child is not already known to the social services authority, then a statement to that effect will be included here, and no additional assessment will have been undertaken.]

Appendix H: Other advice obtained by the authority

[From the Schedule to Regulations 12 and 13 of the Education (Special Educational Needs) Regulations 1994.]

Statement format

The format of the Statement is included at Figure 8.1. This gives the bare bones of the structure of the document, but in helping parents read through the detail, professionals offering support need to alert parents to certain issues. This section gives some suggestions for a critical evaluation of a draft Statement.

The first point to be made is that there are no prizes for getting the contents of a Statement into one side of an A4 sheet of paper. While the Statement should form a succinct summary of the advice, it should also be detailed enough to provide a working basis for action by the school, parents and others involved in supporting the child. Concerns are often expressed by parents and teachers alike that many Statements are too vague, and therefore deemed to be meaningless.

4:26

The Code of Practice indicates that Statements should be clear and unambiguous, use language that both professionals and parents can understand, including explanations of any technical terms used. The gathering of evidence will have taken a considerable amount of effort, resource and time, and a carefully drafted Statement should reflect the same level of professionalism and attention to detail.

Part 1: Introduction

- Home language: if the home language is not English, have the Statement and its appendices been translated into the home language? If not, is there an interpreter available who is trusted by the parents, who can read through the documents with them?

    Even if English is the home language, are the parents sufficiently literate or visually capable of reading the content without further assistance?
- Child's parent or person responsible: if the parents are separated, it should be made clear that both parents have the right to be involved in the decisions about the child's education. This should have been sorted out during the assessment.

Part 2: Special educational needs

In addition to a general statement about a child's overall functioning, this part should specify each of the child's special educational needs that have been identified in the assessment process. It is not sufficient for only the main ones to be included, nor only those needs identified within only one of the appendices. A common complaint by parents is that only the educational psychologist's advice seems to be reflected in the Statement itself. Any needs written in this part of the Statement that are not contained in the advice attached as appendices should be queried, as it implies that the education authority has other advice available that has not been appended. This can often happen where the Named Officer has sought clarification of an element within the advice and received the reply either orally or in the form of an internal memorandum, which may not be classified as a disclosable document. Therefore, any professional asked to clarify their advice during an assessment or during the preparation of a Statement should ensure that the form of reply is disclosable under their own procedures and regulations.

As much as possible, the needs identified in Part 2 should be specific and, where appropriate, quantified. It is insufficient to state that a child 'has difficulties with literacy'; the nature and extent of that difficulty should be detailed, for example by giving a difference between reading and chronological ages.

One very common mistake in this section of the statement results from the ambiguous use of the word 'needs'. In this context, the 'needs' should be the problems, the difficulties, or the factors which prevent the child accessing or fully benefiting from the curriculum. It does not refer to what the child needs in order to make progress; this is provision. For example, the following description is of a need:

X has receptive language difficulties.

The following is not a 'need':

X needs help to understand what is said to him.

This may seem like a highly refined piece of semantics, but in fact it does help to distinguish the child's special needs, or difficulties, from what help – or provision – is required to overcome them. Provision is the province of Part 3.

It would not be unreasonable for Part 2 of the Statement to identify, alongside each need, the source of advice being used. So, for example, an item may read:

X has difficulty with reading, his reading age being 7.6 at chronological age 10.8 [Appendix F].

Any needs identified that are subject to a difference of opinion within the advice attached at the. appendices must be clarified to indicate how the differences are resolved, and the reasons for the conclusions reached. This discussion may not necessarily appear within the wording of the Statement itself, but should be made clear both to the parents and to the parties providing the advice concerned.

Part 3: Special educational provision

4:28

This part differs considerably from the 1983 Regulations Statement that was produced prior to December 1994. Previously, only the provision needed to be specified, together with any National Curriculum implications (since the implementation of the Education Reform Act 1988) but, as can be seen in Figure 8.1, this part now has three clear subsections.

Objectives of provision

This subsection should lay out clearly what the long-term objectives are for the child's educational progress. Linking clearly with the needs identified in Part 2, the objective should be realistic within the expected life of the Statement. (Short-term objectives are a matter for separate discussion.)

For example, if a child cannot write, there could be several different long-term objectives, depending on the severity of the child's difficulties and the prognosis. The objectives could read: 'to enable X to control his pen and trace his name', for a child with severe learning difficulties who may never be expected to achieve functional literacy.

This can be compared to an alternative objective that 'Y should be able to express his ideas clearly in writing at an age-appropriate level' for a child with generally average abilities who for some reason has not gained the equivalent expressive literacy skills. (The reasons should have been identified in the advice, and may be included in Part 2.)

Provision

This subsection should specify the exact provision that should be made to meet each of the needs identified in Part 2. It is good practice to number the 'needs' so that matching numbers can be included under 'provision'. There will inevitably be overlap between the needs, and some elements of provision may meet more than one need; a common example might be the provision of a non-teaching assistant to help to achieve toileting, provide supervision in the playground, and to help to keep the child on task in the classroom. This does not preclude the provisions being identified separately. There are different needs to be met, and in future years, one of the needs might be overcome, allowing its associated provision to be withdrawn. Bundling provisions together only serves to obfuscate this future decision-making process.

Within this part, the Statement should identify which elements of the provision are expected to be provided from within the school's own resources, and which are to be provided additionally by the local education authority. Some education authorities make very specific provisions within a Statement, amounting for example to so many welfare hours, or teaching hours, or specific pieces of equipment. Other authorities provide bandings of budget that are allocated to the school to enable the school to make provision. Whatever the local system, this does not preclude the specification of each provision to be made; any additional resources allocated by the local education authority should be targeted clearly at specific provisions.

In some cases, the local education authority may indicate that no additional resources are to be provided, but that they still intend to maintain a Statement of special educational needs. Parents and schools alike may find this frustrating, wondering why the authority is bothering with a Statement at all. Having undertaken the full assessment, an authority may decide that the child's needs are sufficiently significant to require formal monitoring by them. They may feel that, at the time the Statement was written, no additional resources were required; however, additional provision may be required in the foreseeable future. The annual review process will allow the Statement to be amended so that this provision can be made at the appropriate time. If a Statement were not maintained, a new statutory assessment would be required to determine 'needs' and 'provision' all over again. The 'nil resource' Statement is a more practical means of achieving this end.

Where speech and language therapy is included in Part 3 as an educational provision, the education authority must ensure that the health authority is committed to providing it, and, if this is not possible, must make alternative arrangements for its provision, unless the parents have made their own arrangements.

This subsection of Part 3 will also make reference to any National Curriculum disapplications or modifications.

Monitoring
In the normal course of events, the Statement will be reviewed at least annually. However, there may be elements within the child's needs or provision that warrant other monitoring arrangements.

5:22

This is particularly so in the case of a very young child, where the prediction of future change may be very difficult; it is recommended that Statements for children under five be reviewed informally every six months.

This may also be relevant to a child with a degenerative medical condition, where the needs may change rapidly: or to a medical condition that is undergoing treatment, and may resolve itself or ease considerably within a relatively short space of time. There may be particular elements of the needs that can be expected to change in the light of provisions made available, such as behavioural aspects, and again it is reasonable to expect a modification of the standard review process in such a case.

The monitoring arrangements may specify any particular monitoring procedures such as tests, and any external professionals, such as the educational psychologist or relevant therapist, who will be involved in these procedures.

It is also made clear in the Code of Practice that the school is expected to produce, within two months of the child's placement (or two months of the Statement being finalised if the child is continuing at the same school), a set of short-term targets. These are to be devised in consultation with the child's parents, and being short-term, should be subject to specific review.

Part 4: Placement

4:30

When the proposed Statement is issued, this part will be left blank. Information on types of school or units that may be appropriate, including information on non-maintained special schools, should be provided separately by the local education authority at the same time the proposed Statement is issued. This may be a very long list indeed, and parents may need some assistance in identifying appropriate schools for visiting.

Part 5: Non-educational needs

4:31

The new-style Statement separates, for the first time, educational and non-educational needs. Although old-style Statements (pre-1995) did include a separate section for non-educational provision, the non-educational needs were often included in the section dealing with special educational needs.

What constitutes a non-educational rather than educational need is not clearly defined. Children with physical impairments, requiring physiotherapy or occupational therapy, are generally considered under the Code of Practice to need to have these elements defined as non-educational needs, and anything put in place to meet those needs would be classed as non-educational provision.

For many parents, however, their child's needs in the area of fine and gross motor skills are as important as reading and numeracy. Handling a pen or participating in PE are as vital to accessing the full curriculum as literacy skills are to the dyslexic student, and are required to enable the child to work to the full extent of his or her abilities.

In the case of speech and language difficulties, there is precedence of case law and practice to suggest that, in many cases, speech and language difficulties can be classified as a special *educational* need. This may depend in part on the developmental history of the child, and the nature of the speech and language difficulty. Some local education authorities, for example, will not count as an educational need the speech difficulties a child may suffer as a result of a head injury or other accident, but will include developmental speech or language delay or disorder under Part 2. Different education authorities have different arrangements with their local health authorities to secure the provision of speech and language therapy. However, where this is identified as an educational need, the education authority is responsible for its provision; where it is identified as a non-educational need, the education authority need only ascertain that the health authority will undertake to provide what they feel is required.

It is possible that, over coming years, the case for fine and gross motor skills will also be tested in law. Until then, for the most part the therapies required to overcome these difficulties, such as physiotherapy and occupational therapy, will remain classified as non-educational provision.

Other 'non-educational needs' may include arrangements for respite care, or the need for transport to be provided from home to school.

Part 6: Non-educational provision

4:32 – 4:33

As with Part 3, Part 6 should include any objectives for the provision to meet non-educational needs, as well as the specific provision itself. Also in this part the agency that is to deliver the provision should be identified, and only those elements of provision that have been agreed by other agencies should be included. For example, this part might establish that the health authority will provide physiotherapy, that the social services department will provide respite care, and that the education authority will provide transport.

Although other agencies may be responsible for providing these requirements, the education authority can only include in Parts 5 and 6 those specific items identified in the advice received from the agencies concerned. The education authority should seek to secure some commitment from the other agencies to make the provision before it is committed to in the Statement.

Parents often get angry about the apparent 'buck-passing' that goes on between education and health departments, when issues relating to non-educational needs and provisions are raised. It is important that the relevant specialist from the providing agency take time to clarify any issues that the parents might raise in this regard, and take direct responsibility for the decisions whether or not to make provision. This might be the designated medical officer (DMO) or individual therapist or therapy manager in the case of the health authority; the social work team manager or social worker in the case of the social services department. Where a different officer within the education authority is responsible for the details of a particular non-educational provision, such as transport, the contact details should be made available to the parents so that they can confirm the arrangements directly.

Representations about the content of the Statement

4:65

If parents are in any doubt about the content of the Statement, it is useful for them to state in general terms within the first fifteen days that they disagree with the proposed Statement. This will allow them time subsequently to consider all the points that they may wish to raise. Although parents have only fifteen days in which to state whether or not they agree to the proposed Statement, it may take longer for a meeting to be arranged for their concerns to be discussed.

3:38

In any event, the Code of Practice states that it should take no more than eight weeks before a final Statement is issued. During this time, the parents may seek clarification of any part of the Statement or its appendices, and may meet with officers and other professionals to discuss any disagreements.

It is at this point that it becomes clear that there is considerable benefit in professionals sharing with parents their views, and preferably copies of their reports, during the statutory assessment itself. If parents are faced with all the reports for the first time when they receive the proposed Statement, they may feel overwhelmed at the amount of information they need to take in, and angry that they have not had prior notice of the content of the reports. If differences of opinion are resolved *before* the Named Officer drafts the proposed Statement, then the finalisation of the Statement should be much easier to achieve.

Any professional who has made a contribution to the assessment will need to make themselves available to the parents during the first few weeks after the proposed Statement is issued. If good channels of communication have been set up during the assessment phase, it should not be too difficult to arrange opportunities for discussion at this later stage.

In some cases, it will be necessary to have a multidisciplinary meeting to debate a range of issues within different appendices, and their interpretation by both the Named Officer and the parents. Wherever possible, professionals should try to attend any such meetings, as it is important for the parents to ensure that the Statement that they finally have in place adequately identifies their child's needs and appropriate provisions.

A Statement of Special Educational Needs is in reality a legal document – a contract to which parents are expected to agree, but which they do not sign. It is a contract signed by only one party – the local education authority. It is essential therefore that parents have every opportunity to ensure that they are satisfied with its content.

Naming a school

4:40 – 4:54

In addition to making representations about the content of a Statement, parents are expected to make decisions within this fifteen-day period about which school they might prefer, and state that preference, or make representations for a non-maintained school. If parents have not already been looking at possible schools for their child, this timescale may provoke panic. Even where they have been able to make initial visits to suitable schools, they may want further visits to confirm their initial feelings before committing themselves to a final decision.

Schools – particularly special schools or schools with special units – need to be aware of this time pressure on parents, and be flexible about visiting arrangements. Under the 1981 Education Act, many special schools or schools with special units would only allow parents to visit once that school had been named on a Statement, and the local education authority had referred the papers to the school. While this approach was understandable under the old regulations, which allowed for no parental preference in selecting a school, it is totally inappropriate under the 1993 Education Act and its Code of Practice.

Mainstream schools can assist this decision-making process for parents by ensuring that their SEN policy is readily available, and that either the head teacher or SENCO is willing to meet with prospective parents at relatively short notice. Although in principle each mainstream school is comparable with all other mainstream schools of a similar phase, parents will be seeking out qualitative differences, particularly in the light of the findings of the assessment, and the proposals made in the draft Statement.

Often it is helpful for parents to be able to take the proposed Statement to the school or schools that they are considering, and discuss with each school the way in which they might approach implementing the Statement. This is particularly useful for parents who wish their child to continue attending the same school they already attended when the assessment began. This may be time-consuming for school staff, but provides a very important element of confidence for parents when making their selections.

Where a parent is contemplating a move for their child to a special school or school with a special unit, there may be emotional feelings involved in coming to terms with this significant change. It is important that parents are given a full opportunity to discuss with the staff of the school the nature of the specialist provision available, in the light of the proposed Statement. Wherever possible, special schools and special units may find it useful to put prospective parents in contact with parents of children already attending the school. (See Chapter 4).

All schools, including independent special schools, or independent schools offering specialist provision, have a duty of honesty about their ability to meet the needs of a child as specified in a Statement. Parents are seeking reassurance at this stage in the process that, having identified their child's needs and the appropriate provision, they can rely on the school chosen to meet the commitments contained in the Statement. All too often false reassurance at this stage leads to disappointment and conflict later.

4:56 and 4:41

Parents do not have a right to *choose* which school their child should attend; they have a right to express a preference. The local education authority must comply with the parents' preference of maintained school provided:

- that the school is suitable in age, ability and aptitude to meet the child's special educational needs,
- that the child's attendance is compatible with the efficient education of other children with whom the child would be educated, and
- that such a placement is not incompatible with the efficient use of resources.

122

There are very few grounds on which a school can refuse to accept a child with a Statement of special educational needs.

4:48

There are additional criteria to be met when a parent makes representations about a non-maintained school; in this case, the parent needs to demonstrate that the child's needs cannot be met from within the maintained sector, and that the chosen school can meet the child's special educational needs. If the proposed school is residential, the education authority may ask the social services department to look into the wider needs of the family, for example if the parents are seeking residential placement for respite reasons.

4:49

The Code of Practice recognises that parents need to be given consideration during this decision phase, and suggests the involvement of parent partnership schemes or voluntary organisations that may be able to offer impartial support regarding the benefits of different types of provision, and different schools within the overall type.

The final Statement

4:68 – 4:69

The final Statement should be issued within eight weeks of the initial proposed Statement. It should have incorporated any amendments agreed during the discussion phase after the proposed Statement, and will also name a school in Part 4.

If parents are still dissatisfied with the content of Parts 2, 3 or 4 of the Statement, they can appeal to the SEN tribunal (see Chapter 10).

Assuming the final Statement is satisfactory, the next step for parents is to ensure that it is implemented.

Implementing the Statement

There is little that is more frustrating to parents than to plough through the identification, referral, assessment and Statementing procedures, perhaps taking up to a year altogether (in the past, sometimes longer) only to find that, once the Statement is agreed, the new school admitting the child for the first time as a result of the Statement then proceeds to use the first term to 'assess the child's needs'.

It is particularly annoying if the parents have taken time to ensure that the advice provided by the professionals during the assessment accurately reflects their child's needs, and if they have met with officers and professionals to ensure that the wording of the Statement is an accurate reflection of that advice, and the provision specified is appropriate and relevant to meet the needs.

> The teaching staff appear to read the Statement but seem to need to do reassessments to prove the findings. Consequently they seem surprised when asked what is being done about certain things – particularly when the problem hasn't been picked up by them.

> (Mrs X whose son has language delay, learning difficulties and behavioural problems.)

While most parents would recognise that a new school will need to evaluate the precise nature of the delivery of any special provision, as well as taking some time to set shorter-term targets required under Part 3 of the Statement, they are often very unhappy about no effective provision being put in place until another lengthy school assessment has been completed. The two months set out in the Code for the school to set short-term targets is a maximum, not a prescription. If the new school feels that such a new assessment is necessary, they should explain to the parents the reasons for it, together with the proposed timescale. Anything that can be done to shorten this delay should be done.

4:75

Schools should establish a policy regarding who in the school reads a Statement once it is finalised, and how all the staff involved with the child are to be prepared for his or her arrival (or continued provision). At the very least, the SENCO (if in a mainstream school), the head teacher, the child's form or class teacher and the designated governor should read the Statement. If a welfare assistant or special tutor is to be involved, they should also be given the opportunity to understand the content of the Statement, and the reasons for their own involvement. Other staff teaching the child should be made aware of the child's needs and any special provision that is available.

If the school can arrange it, parents may prefer to attend a meeting with the relevant staff in school to go through the final Statement looking at the individual requirements, and ensuring a full understanding of the child's needs as described in the Statement and attached advice. When parents come into school, or contact the school, regarding their child's day-to-day needs, they prefer to know that the staff who deal with their child, and who are available to talk with them, do understand their child's needs. All too often, a Statement is finalised, sent to the school and filed in the child's individual record, without any of the staff dealing directly with the child having the opportunity to read, understand or discuss its content. Often this has been due to the fact that Statements have been regarded as too vague. Sometimes it is due to lack of time. However, time taken at the outset to understand the child's needs will save time and distress later on for both the child and the professionals, as meeting the child's needs is designed to minimise problems.

Any disclosure of the Statement, however, must be in the interests of the child, and all who read it or are party to discussion of its content must bear in mind that it is a confidential document.

Parents frequently complain that specific provision identified in the Statement is not being made in the classroom. They will not necessarily be content with the answer that 'the professional judgement' of the classroom staff overrides the provisions outlined in the Statement. Any variation of provision within the school from that specified in the Statement must be discussed with parents before implementation. It may be that an interim adjustment is justified following an improvement in progress, prior to the formal annual review; but it must not be allowed just 'to happen' without open and deliberate decisions taking place.

Liaison between school staff and other outside specialists offering support or therapy programmes to children in school is another frequent cause of complaint by parents. In many cases, the parents have known and trusted the therapists for many years before the Statement was finalised, and before the child was admitted to the school. Under these circumstances, any perceived blocking of the therapist's work by the school staff is likely to cause considerable unease and possible conflict between the parents and the school. Schools may set out in their SEN policy a general framework for working with outside professionals, but should also agree specific arrangements in the child's individual plan for external specialists involved with implementing the child's Statement. In particular, if new medical needs arise after the Statement is implemented, the school should seek to work with the parents in accessing appropriate advice and, if necessary, securing an amendment to Parts 5 and 6 of the Statement.

If parents feel that the school is not implementing the Statement in full, they should be encouraged to speak with either the head teacher or, in the case of a mainstream school, the SENCO, to begin discussions on how best to resolve the matter. The school's own complaints procedure should also be made available for the parent without prejudice to their position or that of their child.

In fact, the local education authority retains responsibility for ensuring that the Statement is implemented, and parents may contact their Named Officer to discuss their complaint, without necessarily using the school's own complaints procedures. This is the due process, and schools should not see such a move by the parents as being hostile to the school. Significant variations in delivery of provision within the school compared to that specified in the Statement should only be carried out after full review and after an amended Statement has been issued.

Once the child is admitted to the school, particularly if this is a special school, the parents will need continued reassurance and access to staff. Many children at special school are not delivered or collected by their parents, and so home/school liaison must be a priority. Where it is implemented, parents do appreciate the effort that staff make.

> The classroom teacher was very helpful and pleased to help personally or over the phone. The head teacher at our son's school is very supportive both practically phoning and arranging for our son to start school and with his transport, arranging extra dance therapy which is not on his Statement but is provided by the school anyway. They are lovely and his class teacher has given us her home phone number and is always available to speak to.
>
> (Mrs T whose son attends a special nursery.)

Practical points

- *Form/class teachers*: Read the Statements for every child in your class or form. Make sure that any classroom or welfare assistants understand their role in the child's provision based on the advice in the Statement.
- *Subject teachers*: Be aware of the needs of any child in the class who may be subject to a Statement. Check with the SENCO when taking over a new class. The SENCO should advise on any child who is newly subject to a Statement. Be aware of how any new difficulties can be reported to the SENCO, particularly if the child seems to need additional help.
- *SENCOs*: Examine carefully any draft Statement issued to which the school has submitted advice. If there are any discrepancies, make this known to the parents, and if possible to the Named Officer. Try to make time to discuss the draft Statement with the parents of a child already at your school. Be willing to meet with parents who may be looking for a new school for their child once the draft Statement has been issued. Develop suitable contacts among parents of children with

Statements already at the school, who can speak to prospective parents. Make sure that every member of staff teaching the child is aware of the fact that the child has a Statement.

- *Head teachers*: Examine carefully any draft Statement issued to which the school has submitted advice. If there are any discrepancies, make this known to the parents, and if possible to the Named Officer.
- *Governors*: Ensure that the school has suitable arrangements for prospective parents with draft Statements to visit the school at short notice. Check arrangements for SENCOs and class or subject teachers to familiarise themselves with final Statements.
- *Psychologists and other contributors to the appended advice*: Examine carefully any draft Statement issued to which you have submitted advice. If there are any discrepancies, make this known to the parents, and if possible to the Named Officer. Be prepared to make time to see parents who wish to discuss the content of the Statement or the advice attached to it.
- *External specialists involved in provision in school*: Ensure there are clear guidelines for working in the school, regarding where the work is to be carried out, at what time, and how any advice or programmes are to be communicated to school staff and parents.
- *Named Officers*: Ensure that the Statement accurately reflects the advice received, and that all advice is attached to the Statement before it is sent. Be prepared to arrange meetings at short notice to include other professionals as necessary.

9 Annual reviews

Section 172(5), 1993 Education Act

Every Statement of special educational needs must be reviewed at least annually. It can be reviewed at any time within the year if it is felt that the child's needs have changed or that the provision required to meet the needs should be altered. Review of the Statement will also include review of any school-generated plan of shorter-term targets, and any previously developed Transition Plan for a child over fourteen years of age (see later in this chapter).

The annual review is an annual review of the Statement; it is not merely a review of the child's progress. Schools should ensure that feedback on the child's educational and non-educational progress is provided throughout the school year, and should not rely solely on the annual review to undertake this. As with any child in mainstream school, there should be an opportunity for the parents to attend routine parent consultations with staff teaching their child. These do, however, need to be handled sensitively by the teaching staff, particularly in those consultations that are easily overheard by other parents and staff. No matter how well supported their child is through the implementation of a Statement, parents will still feel very sensitive about their own child's 'differentness' compared to others in the class, group or school.

Where there are special concerns about how a child might progress under the implementation of a Statement, consideration should be given to more frequent, less formal consultations when parents can be brought up to date with developments. This is particularly important where parents are involved in the special support for their child at home, perhaps through homework supervision, additional work, or behaviour management programmes.

An examination of the short-term targets set after the finalisation of the Statement will indicate whether more frequent consultations and reviews might be required. While it would be impractical for parents to attend every internal discussion held in a school about their child, there should always be an agreed mechanism for informing the parents of any outcome from such discussion, and an opportunity provided for the parents to come into school to discuss the matter.

Many special schools do not hold parent consultations as a regular event, relying on the annual review to report on progress or necessary changes. The nature of the annual review under the Code of Practice, however, makes it more important than ever that parents have an opportunity to review how their child is progressing in school *before* the annual review process takes place. They will have an opportunity to submit their own ideas to the review, preferably in time for their report to be circulated along with others two weeks before the meeting. Parents will appreciate and benefit from consultation with the staff before making their own comments in writing.

The annual review is a process, not a single event on a particular day. The review meeting is the focus of the review process, but parents need to be involved in the preparation for that meeting as well as in the consideration of the outcome. An annual review may result in an amended Statement, which means that parents have all the same rights to involvement, representation and appeal as they do for the first Statement.

Parents have often expressed dismay that their views have not been taken into account in annual reviews in the past. This may have happened because they were not invited to attend the review meeting or participate in the process; or they may feel that although they were allowed to state their views, no one was really prepared to listen to them. The way in which parental views are taken into account is as important as the fact that they are taken into account.

6:7

Preparation for the annual review begins when the local education authority notifies the school that the review is required. The school should receive such notification at least two months prior to the review report being due. This will therefore provide approximately six weeks between the authority notifying the school, and the review meeting itself. If the school or the parents feel that an earlier review is required, they need to notify the education authority so that the process can be initiated by them.

Parents need as much time as possible to prepare for their involvement in the annual review process and the meeting itself. It is helpful therefore if the school, on receiving notification that the annual review is due, contact the parents directly to arrange a suitable date and time for the meeting. For many working parents, shorter notice may make attendance at the meeting inconvenient or impossible.

The ideal procedure would include giving the parents a brief summary of the purpose of the review, and of the process to be undertaken; this might include timing of any re-assessments, psychologist's observations, circulation of reports and arrangements for the meeting itself. This will enable parents to prepare appropriately for the meeting rather than just turn up to hear what the professionals have to say.

It may be that external specialists will be asked to have an input to the review, and within reason, parents should be asked to consider whether there are any additional specialists who should be consulted or invited to attend the meeting. It may be that the child has been seeing other professionals outside school, and their reports may be of value in the review itself. This might particularly be the case where a child has been undergoing treatment for a long-term medical condition and has the opportunity for a review appointment at the hospital or clinic.

Any therapists who have been involved in providing direct therapy or who have devised programmes for delivery within the school should be asked to submit a review report, in time for circulation prior to the meeting. It is essential that the school check at the outset who has been involved, and that all relevant reports are requested in time for circulation. This sometimes fails to happen, as in the case of L, a girl with cerebral palsy, who has a Statement and is educated in mainstream school. When the parents were sent the papers for L's annual review, there was no report from the occupational therapist or the physiotherapist, both of whom visited L regularly in school, and both of whom had contributed to the Statement. When Mother questioned this, the SENCO indicated that she was not aware that these professionals had any involvement.

Again, parents may wish to meet with these therapists before any reports are compiled, or between the reports being circulated and the review meeting, particularly if the therapist concerned is unable to attend the meeting.

Parents often feel annoyed if they are unable to meet the various professionals who deal with their child. There is a feeling that schools sometimes behave as if the specialists – for example, speech and language therapists – are serving the school, and therefore are accountable only directly to the school. This is an inappropriate view of the working relationship. The child is the 'client' and the parents, as the individuals responsible for the welfare of the child, are therefore entitled to direct access to these professionals.

6:12

It is accepted that it may not always be possible for all the professionals concerned with a child to attend every single review meeting. For this reason, it is appropriate for the head teacher to meet with the parents at the start of the review process, to discuss which professionals should be invited. The school must invite any professional suggested by the education authority in the notification for the annual review, but this does not preclude others being involved.

It is good practice to ensure that the educational psychologist is involved on a regular basis, even if this does not happen every year. Parents will need to ensure that the psychological advice is up to date, particularly for reviews that precede decisions about transfer between phases, or other decisions to change the placement. Between those events, the head teacher should consider the benefit of involving the educational psychologist perhaps every two or three years. In the past, some children have proceeded throughout their primary education, having acquired their first Statement at the age of five, with no updated psychological advice being sought. Clearly the developments a child goes through over that period of time will render the original psychological advice invalid for decisions made towards secondary transfer. The local education authority may have an overall policy on the minimum frequency with which a psychologist should see a child who is subject to a Statement, and headteachers and SENCOs should ensure they are aware of that policy.

As with the original Statement, parents may wish to submit evidence to the review from independent specialists who know their child. Although not specifically allowed for in the Code of Practice, wherever possible schools should welcome this additional advice as being complementary to that available from those directly involved through the Statement.

Parents may feel the same difficulties in making a submission to the annual review as they did making a contribution to the statutory assessment (see Chapter 7). In particular, if they feel that some things are not going particularly well, they may be reluctant to appear critical of the school, especially where the school is making excellent provision in all other respects. In this case, the head teacher and/or SENCO should seek to reassure parents that any criticism will not jeopardise the working relationship between school and home, and encourage an honest exchange of views.

6:16

It may be appropriate to direct parents to a relevant voluntary organisation that can help them compile their own report, or who will send a supporter to the review meeting to help the parents make an oral contribution. Many parents are reluctant to get involved in any formal way; they might not have made any contribution to their child's statutory assessment or Statement, and so be unused to looking critically at their child's abilities and progress. Their participation in annual reviews, however, can contribute to the ongoing relationship with the school and can help to consolidate the good working partnership between teaching staff and home.

Schools may like to offer some written information for parents about the annual review, and Figure 9.1 gives an outline of the type of information that could be included.

Figure 9.1

Guidance for parents – annual reviews

1. When the review is notified

Ensure that the meeting date is convenient for you to attend. Contact the head teacher of the school if there are any difficulties with the suggested date.

2. Who will be involved?

In addition to yourselves as parents, the school staff teaching your child, and the head teacher, other professionals will be invited for their views, including:
[Here write in the names and titles of any other professionals to be involved]
They may not be able to attend the meeting, but the following have been invited:
[Here write in the names of those being invited to the meeting.]
If there are any other specialists who have been seeing your child recently, who may have a view on his or her progress, talk to the head teacher [or SENCO] about involving them also.

3. Preparing for the review

Your views are important. If possible we would like you to let us have your views in writing so that they can be circulated to everyone involved before the meeting. You will also receive copies of everyone else's reports two weeks before the meeting.
If you don't feel confident writing your views down, contact *[head teacher or SENCO]* who can arrange to meet with you to discuss your views and write them down for you. Alternatively, you may find it helpful to contact *[name of appropriate voluntary organisation]* or the Named Person identified to you when your child's final Statement was issued *[if appropriate]*.

4. Writing your report

You may find it helpful to look through your copy of the Statement, and any review reports which you have received, so that you can compare your child's progress now against those documents. In particular:
- *Needs:* have your child's needs changed? Which needs have improved, which are still the same, and which, if any, are worse? Are there any new needs which are not on the current Statement?
- *Provision:* does the provision included in the Statement meet the needs of your child? Is it too much, or too little? Is it the wrong sort of help?
- *Placement:* is this still the right school for your child, or are there circumstances which might require a different school (for example, secondary transfer)?

It is also helpful to look through your copy of the short-term targets set by the school after the last Statement or review. Check if there are any changes needed for the coming year.

Figure 9.1 continued

---

5. Reading the reports

About two weeks before the review meeting, you will be sent copies of all the reports which the various professionals have prepared and will discuss at the review meeting. When you receive these reports, if there is anything you do not understand, contact the professional concerned, or the head teacher [*or SENCO*] to discuss it.

As you read the reports, make notes of anything which you will want to discuss at the meeting.

6. At the review meeting

If you feel that you might need help, you may bring along a friend to the meeting. This might be your Named Person. Please let the head teacher know before the meeting if you will be bringing someone else along. If you think you will want an interpreter, or signer, please let the school know as soon as possible so that this can be arranged.

Make sure you have a chance to ask all the questions you have prepared. If during the meeting there is anything you do not understand, please ask for an explanation.

7. What happens after the meeting?

After the meeting, the head teacher will write a review report including any new targets agreed, and will send this to the LEA and everyone involved in the review. The LEA will then decide whether there needs to be any changes to the Statement, and may issue a proposed amended Statement, which they will send to you for your agreement. After this, a final amended Statement may be issued.

8. What if I don't agree with the amended Statement?

You have the same rights of appeal to the SEN tribunal as with the original Statement. If this is required, you will be able to ask for a leaflet on how to appeal.

Preparing reports with parents in mind

Annual review reports must be as honest and unbiased as the assessment reports and advice that contribute to the initial Statement. Too often, the reports prepared by schools appear to give either too good or too dismal a picture of a child's progress.

Too good to be true?

Schools often wish to give parents considerable amounts of reassurance about their child's progress and happiness at school. For this reason, reports often accentuate the positive, which in itself is not a bad thing. The difficulties arise when *all* the information is 'positive' and there appear to be no difficulties whatsoever for the child in school. Parents are happy that their child seems to be doing so well, but begin to get suspicious, and even depressed, if everything is made to look too rosy.

> Every report we got made W seem like a complete angel. She never had a tantrum, could eat properly and drink from a cup, knew how to count to five, and chose books from the library. She always did what she was told and never gave any cheek. I know the school were trying to make us feel good, but in fact it had the opposite effect. If she could eat properly at school, why wouldn't she eat properly at home? When I tried to give her a drink in a cup, it went down the front of her clothes. She would throw a tantrum in the middle of the supermarket, and wouldn't be seen dead with a book. Where was *I* going wrong? If the teachers could get her to do these things, why couldn't I? It made me feel like a lousy parent.
>
> (Mrs I, mother of W, who attends an SLD school.)

Do problems mean resources?

The converse of this scenario is the report that exaggerates the child's difficulties, so that the local education authority will continue to provide the level of resource, or possibly increase it, to help the school support the child's provision.

> They kept telling me he was a danger in the playground, that he needed constant supervision in class, and that the full-time welfare helper was still needed. I went along with it, believing N was never going to gain any kind of independence. It was only after a couple of years I realised that the school was just trying to make sure that the LEA still paid for the full-time welfare helper. In fact, N rarely needed supervision, and the welfare helper was off helping other children, in other classrooms, for half the time.
>
> (Mrs K, whose son N successfully integrated into mainstream primary from special school.)

What is important to remember is that parents read any report on their child with a subjective and personal slant. This does not mean the reports need sanitising, just that they need to be honest, easy to understand, unambiguous and sensitive in the language used.

If the parents' first language is not English, consider having the key documents translated, or provide an opportunity before the meeting itself for the parents to meet with an interpreter who can explain their content.

134

The outcome of a review may be a recommendation that the Statement be amended, resulting in possible changes in descriptions of the child's needs, the provision or the placement. Too often, annual reviews are held that concentrate only on the provision, and particularly on the additional resources being provided by the local education authority for the school. While this is a legitimate element of the annual review, parents need to know that their child is the focus of the review, and not the authority's funding. Parents often get drawn into the debate between the education authority and school regarding 'who funds?', when in fact they should not need to be party to this, as the question of funding is purely an administrative matter within the system.

Very few parents are used to participating in large-scale meetings with professionals, and head teachers in particular can do much to place the parents at ease. These suggestions might help:

- Meet with the parents immediately before the meeting, without other professionals being present, to discuss the way the meeting will be conducted, and how the parents' own views will be included.
- Be clear at the start of the meeting if there is a limited amount of time available. It is particularly important to check whether any of the external specialists attending will need to leave early, so that their views can be sought in the earlier part of the meeting, and parents given an opportunity to clarify anything in their reports.
- Check with the parents if they have a list of questions they would like to ask. It might be appropriate for all the questions that the parents have prepared to be listed at the outset, and addressed as each relevant part of the discussion is reached. This avoids a common problem, that parents have a question they would like to ask, but find it difficult to interrupt the flow of the discussion, thus missing their opportunity.
- After each professional has presented their report (if that is the format of the meeting), ask the parents first if there are any questions on that particular report they would like to ask, or points they would like clarified.
- When all the discussion has finished, ask the parents again if there is anything else they would like to say or ask.
- Make a clear summary of the discussions, and outline the next stage of the procedure: when the review report will be ready, and who will receive it; when the local education authority is expected to complete its consideration of the review report.

Taking into account the child's views

As with the statutory assessment, this can be a difficult area. However, any child has the right to express their view on their own progress and, subject to their age and ability to understand, these views should be taken into account during the annual review process. It should be agreed at the outset with the parents how the child's views are to be elicited and recorded. It might involve a two-part approach in both school and home.

If there is a member of staff in the school with whom the child has built a trusting relationship, it may be possible for this person to act as the 'scribe' or 'facilitator' for the child. If the child is able to write or otherwise record his or her own views, they should be given some guidance and possible headings to work to, as well as the opportunity to discuss what they have written or said with an adult at school and at home.

Parents are not trained in interviewing their children, and children are often eager to provide their parents with the answers they think their parents want. Sometimes the converse can occur, when children seek to give the opposite answer to that which they know is sought. This does not mean that parents are therefore unsuited to the task of helping their child express his or her own views. Rather, parents themselves need support in doing this.

Open, general questions have to be treated with caution, as do leading questions: for example, 'Are you happy at school?' is so vague as to be useless, while 'You like Mrs Bloggs, the support teacher, don't you?' is too directional. Care should be taken, particularly with a young or sensitive child, that involvement in the review does not heighten their own perceptions of their own difficulties.

Once the child's views have been recorded, time must be spent in the review meeting to discuss these. In the review report, clear acknowledgement should be made of the child's views as separate from those of the parents and professionals.

If the child is of sufficient age and understanding, consideration should be given to allowing the child to participate in the annual review meeting itself, either for part of the time or for the whole time. Some parts of the discussion may not be suitable for the child to witness, and often parents feel uncomfortable talking about their child's difficulties openly in front of them.

Wherever the child has been encouraged to submit their own views, there must be an agreed process for informing the child of the outcome of the meeting's discussions. Even where the child has not been involved in the preparation for, or attendance at, the meeting, consideration should be given to providing an opportunity to discuss the review with the child before the final report is submitted to the local education authority. It should not be assumed that the parents will want or know how to address this issue with their child. Agreement beforehand and at the meeting on how this should be done will be required.

Once the review meeting is over, the Code of Practice requires that the review report that is sent to the local education authority by the head teacher should also be circulated to all involved. It is important that the parents receive a copy at the earliest opportunity, so that they can be sure that their views have been appropriately represented. This is not because head teachers are likely deliberately to misrepresent the views expressed by the parents, but because parents are generally unused to participating in formal meetings, and may not have clearly articulated their concerns or views. Only by reading the formal report of the review meeting will parents be able to identify where they may not have expressed themselves clearly, or where they missed an opportunity to speak up. They can then put this right by discussing the matter with the head teacher, or writing to the authority to clarify any particular points.

14+ reviews

Parents need to know what is likely to happen during an annual review when their child is fourteen, and how that might differ from other reviews. Of particular concern to many parents is the statutory involvement of the social services department. This agency can often have negative connotations for parents, and they may be suspicious of the reasons for their appearance at this stage. Parents of children with emotional and/or behavioural difficulties may be particularly fearful of the involvement of social services in the 14+ review.

Some parents are unsure about the involvement of the careers service at the age of fourteen. They may feel there is extra pressure for their child to be moved out of the school system, and away from the 'protection' of the local education authority and Statement that has been so essential in enabling their child to progress so far.

As with so many other elements of the parent partnership, information and time are paramount. Clear information about the nature of the 14+ review, provided both by the education authority and the school, should be combined with an opportunity for parents to discuss the implications of the more detailed review taking place.

The Transition Plan

Many parents indicate from quite an early stage that they are concerned about the options for their child's future after leaving school. In the recent survey conducted by the author (see Appendix A), parents of children as young as eleven were expressing concern about 16+ options. By the time their child reaches fourteen, this concern is very real indeed, and there is often bewilderment about the options and how provision can be accessed. Difficult and stressful though the Statementing process may be, the apparent lack of an overall system to cover assessment for special college provision, and the widening split between education and other agencies, presents parents with considerable anxiety.

Schools that have a large number of children with special educational needs, including those at Stage Three, should acquaint themselves with the details of local further education establishments and colleges further afield that may be able to meet students' special needs. Careers teachers within schools should ensure that information is readily available, not only to the students but also to the parents, about the way the further education system operates, and, wherever possible, offer to act as a contact point to signpost parents to appropriate contacts at local colleges.

The careers service is expected to be involved in the 14+ review, and for students whose post-16 options clearly require specialist intervention in education and training, special needs careers officers should seek to develop a positive working relationship both with the student and his or her parents. For many parents, this part of the evaluation may represent the first time that their child has been involved separately in the decision-making.

> We'd been so used, over the years, to making all the decisions for N that we sort of assumed the same procedures would follow with the careers service. N had been asked for his views before, or been in meetings with professionals, but never on his own. The careers officer came into reception and asked N to follow her into the interview room. When we got up to follow, she said 'No, I'll see you later.' It was nerve-wracking! It was only then I realised that N was going to have to start making life decisions, and in fact this was a very good start.

(Mrs K, whose son N has Asperger syndrome.)

6:59

The Code of Practice makes particularly clear that the student should be actively involved in the development of the Transition Plan. All the caveats about children's participation in assessments and annual reviews still apply at the 14+ review. While many pupils will have reached a greater

138

understanding of their own needs and the provision made to meet them, others may be unable to project into the world beyond school, and will require considerable assistance in making suitably informed choices. Professionals involved with the family, whether they are teachers, careers officers, social workers or psychologists, need to be particularly sensitive to the feelings of parents at this stage in their child's maturity.

Parents are torn by conflicting wishes for and on behalf of their children as they approach the end of their formal school education and begin to consider the range of future options. On the one hand they want their child to become as independent as possible, and on the other they wish to extend their protection of them. This is true of all parents, whether or not their child has special needs. The feelings are exaggerated, however, where the pupil has special needs. The parents have probably fought many battles both within the home and with external agencies over the years to maximise their child's independence. The approach of adulthood in their child may be a time when early hopes are finally dashed, or where the hopes being realised actually cause an onset of panic.

I don't want her to leave home, but I know she will have to; I want her to move on from school, but am scared that the right provision isn't available. I look back over all these years and wonder what we've really achieved. But then I know that we – well, she has achieved an awful lot. I'm not very good at expressing it: I think the head teacher was rather shocked when I said that the first priority was to get my daughter away from her mother!

(Mrs A, mother of eighteen-year-old I, who had attended an SLD school since the age of four.)

Outcomes of annual review

For most children, most annual reviews will result in an acknowledgement of achievement, and possibly a reduction in special provision as specified in the Statement. New targets will be set for the coming year, or period to the next review if it is to take place sooner.

From the advice received in the review report, the local education authority will determine whether any changes are required to the Statement. Parents need to be made aware during the review process that the authority may issue an amended Statement as a result of the review. Changes may be made to any part of the Statement, and parents must be alert to the likely implications of changes in needs or changes in provision being specified. An amended Statement may also specify a change in school, such as for phase transfer, or from mainstream to special placement, or vice versa.

Parents have the same rights to make representations about an amended Statement following review as they do about an initial proposed (or draft) Statement. They must make these representations within fifteen days of receiving the proposal to amend the Statement. The education authority has to consider any parental representations and explain their reasons for not complying if a final amended Statement is issued without further change. The final amended Statement must be issued within eight weeks of any proposal to amend the Statement.

Where parents dispute the final amended Statement, they have the same rights of appeal to the SEN Tribunal; this applies to disputes over Parts 2, 3 and 4 of the Statement.

The local education authority may decide, on considering the review report, that a Statement is no longer required. If this decision is made, then the authority must write to the parents explaining the decision, and providing copies of any evidence taken into account when making that decision. The review meeting itself may have concluded that the Statement was no longer required and, with the agreement of the parents involved at the meeting, made that proposal to the authority. In these circumstances, the school should have already explained to the parents what provision will be in place, and what monitoring arrangements are to be made, to support the pupil after the Statement has ceased.

Where parents disagree with a decision to cease to maintain a Statement, they have the right to appeal to the SEN tribunal.

Although not specifically allowed for in the Code of Practice, it would be appropriate for the school to maintain a child at Stage Three for at least a term after the Statement has ceased, and at Stage Two for another term, before removing all support and monitoring completely. This allows for external advisers to be called upon to ensure an appropriate IEP is in place following the Statement, and that the provision is gradually wound down rather than withdrawn completely and suddenly.

Practical points

- *Teachers*: Be prepared to offer an informal meeting with the parents to discuss how the child is progressing, before the review meeting.
- *Head teachers*: Check with the parents that the date for the review meeting is acceptable. Offer help to the parents in compiling their own contribution. Ensure all reports are circulated two weeks before the meeting. Help the parents participate in the meeting. Summarise the review meeting verbally before closing. Consider ensuring that non-teaching assistants and any support tutors are available to talk with the parents, even if they cannot be at the meeting.

- *SENCOs*: Be prepared to offer help to parents to encourage participation. Check that all teachers are aware of the review, and co-ordinate reports from all staff working with the child.
- *Professionals providing advice*: Ensure that your review report is submitted in time to be circulated before the meeting. Be prepared to meet with the parents to discuss any details of the report, particularly if you are unable to attend the meeting.
- *Named Officers*: Be clear about the process and timescales for reviews. For 14+ reviews, ensure the parents are encouraged to participate, and be sensitive to their concerns about other agencies being involved and about transition.
- *SEN careers officers*: Be aware that many parents find the initial careers interview daunting, as the first real indication that their child will soon move on out of the school system.
- *Social workers*: Be sensitive to concerns parents may have about your involvement if it is for the first time.

10 Complaints and appeals

Parents do not like complaining. They often feel that the process of complaining will only serve to make matters worse, that they will be seen as 'troublemakers' and that as a result their child may suffer. Complaining about the process may reflect badly on those individuals within the system that they have come to trust. Thus parents are always faced with a dilemma.

> The DMO saw A at a normal school visit and based his report solely on that visit without including other medical information or the speech therapist's report. The EP assessed A without giving us the opportunity to be present and did ask some colleagues to see A without our knowledge. We see the EP as a strong ally and would not wish to complain about this for fear of upsetting the relationship.
>
> (Mrs K whose son A is profoundly deaf.)

The parents who do complain or take their case to appeal are only a minority of the parents who feel some dissatisfaction about the way their child's special educational needs have been addressed. Far more hide their dissatisfaction from the school or authority, in the fear that the professionals about whom they would complain will 'take it out' on their child. By so suppressing their real feelings, they can jeopardise the working relationship that is so essential to their child's well-being.

By the time parents do reach the point of making an actual complaint or lodging an appeal, they have often gone beyond conciliation. Complaints and appeals procedures need to take account of this.

Complaints about schools' decisions or actions

2:10

The Code of Practice and the 1994 SEN (Information) Regulations require schools to develop a complaints procedure for parents as part of the school's SEN policy. The Parent's Guide expands on this.

Where parents feel the need to make a complaint about the way their child has been treated, within the general area of his or her special educational needs, the complaints procedure must be clear and allow a maximum degree of independence and impartiality to be brought to bear on the discussions, particularly from the school's side. This may be extremely difficult in a small primary school, where the class teacher, SENCO and head teacher may be seen by the parents as working very closely together, and as a result may be perceived by the parent as colluding or conspiring together in defence against the complaint.

As with so many other areas of interaction between the parents and professionals, the absence of such collusion is insufficient; it is the perception of the *apparent* collusion that is important. If it is felt that parents are so mistrustful, consideration should be given to asking an independent individual to facilitate a meeting between the school staff concerned and the parents. This might be the designated governor or chair of governors. In a larger secondary school, it may be possible to recruit another member of staff who is not directly involved with the child and can be seen as impartial. If a house system operates, the head of house, or in extreme cases the head of another house, may be a useful source of this impartiality.

The role of the governing body should be made absolutely clear in the complaints procedures. Parents who are feeling disgruntled about the way a school is handling their complaint may not believe that the governing body is impartial, and may expect the governors to 'side with the head teacher'. Consideration should be given to how this perception might be overcome as a policy before any individual complaint arises.

Parents should be told to whom they can complain if they are dissatisfied with the outcome of the school-based complaints procedures, preferably at the outset, so that they are clear that there is recourse beyond the school.

It is a paradox that the best way to avoid complaints is to encourage them. It is a lesson that has been learnt in the world of retailing and commerce, and one that could readily be adopted within the education system. Many of the most successful businesses thrive on the benefits they gain from their customers' complaints. They learn how to improve their service or products; they can enhance the loyalty of the customer who complains by good and prompt handling of the complaint; and the customer who has complained and been well dealt with will act as an advocate in the future.

Complaints about LEA procedures and personnel

Those local education authorities that have set up proactive complaints or appeals procedures have also benefited. One authority that set up an independent conciliation service soon earned the respect of parents and parent representatives. It was seen to be impartial, and officers within the conciliation service were perceived as objective as well as 'user-friendly'.

Decisions reached were generally well received by the parents, whether or not they were in the parents' favour. The complaints procedure was not seen as prejudicial to the ongoing working relationship between the parties.

The reputation of a good and effective complaints process soon spreads. When parents begin to feel confident in the complaints procedures, they will inevitably complain more. However, they are likely to complain sooner, when their concerns are relatively minor and positions have not become entrenched on either side. School staff should be encouraged to adopt a positive attitude to complaints, as should education authority officers and other professionals.

SEN tribunal

The SEN tribunal was devised to answer the criticism that the old appeal system was neither fair nor seen to be fair. Parents had little or no faith in the process and believed that it was designed to work against them.

> I wrote consistently and the LEA became more entrenched. I was advised to go to appeal. I did not as I knew that what I was asking for had been my son's right in law for more than ten years and that I had said this enough times without having to commit more time, energy and expense to a system that was likely to abuse us further.
>
> (Mrs T, whose son has Down's syndrome.)

Under the pre-tribunal appeal system, parents had no right to appeal if the local education authority decided not to assess their child. The rights of appeal only began once the assessment had begun.

The old appeal system was two-tier: first came a local appeals committee, set up by the local authority against whose decision the parents were appealing; the second level was appeal to the Secretary of State. Even if the local appeal committee found in favour of the parents, their decisions were not binding. They could not change the content of the Statement, only ask the authority to reconsider its content. By the end of that system, appeal to the Secretary of State was taking anything up to two years to process.

The SEN tribunal was introduced to allow for a single appeal process, the findings of which are binding on all parties, and against whose decision there is no further automatic right of appeal.[1]

Parents gained the right to appeal to the SEN tribunal against any relevant decision made by the education authority on or after 1 September

---

[1] Either party to the tribunal can appeal to the High Court against the tribunal's decision, but only on points of law.

1994. By early January 1995, 250 appeals had been lodged. The first tribunal hearing was held on 19 January 1995. It is estimated that the rate of appeals will increase quite rapidly over time.

Parents have the right to appeal to the SEN tribunal if:

- they disagree with the education authority's decision not to assess *and they, the parents, have been involved in requesting the assessment;*
- after completing a statutory assessment, the education authority refuses to issue a Statement;
- they disagree with the content of Part 2 (special educational needs), Part 3 (special educational provision) or Part 4 (placement) of the final Statement or final amended Statement;
- the education authority refuses to reassess the child's special educational needs (and the parents' request was made more than six months after any previous assessment);
- they disagree with the education authority's decision to cease to maintain a Statement.

Only parents may appeal to the SEN tribunal.

By the time a parent feels the need to take their case to a formal, statutory appeal, they are likely to have exhausted all available routes to resolution of their differences of opinion with the local education authority. This was recognised by the Department for Education when they set up the tribunals, and a great deal of effort was put in to establish a system that attempted to minimise that confrontation.

The proceedings of the SEN tribunal are intended to be informal, parent-friendly and unbiased. It was not envisaged that tribunal hearings should be adversarial or populated with lawyers. Although it has always been acknowledged as a 'legal' process, its proceedings were to be jargon free and executed in as conciliatory a manner as possible. It was not the intention that the tribunal hearings would be like courts of law, nor that legal representation of parents or education authorities should become the norm.

As this book is being prepared, only a few tribunal hearings have been held, but initial indications are that they are rapidly becoming more adversarial and are including a higher level and frequency of legal representation than was originally envisaged by the Department for Education or the president of the tribunal.

When the SEN tribunal was first proposed, there was an attempt to secure an agreement by local education authorities that they would not use lawyers if the parents were themselves not represented by lawyers during the hearing itself. This 'concordat' failed, as authorities reserved the right to use all available resources to defend their own decisions. In the event, it appears that a significant number of parents lodging appeals are using lawyers anyway. Parents are aware that the tribunal's decision is binding; they feel that they cannot afford to increase the risk of losing, and so are keen wherever possible to use a lawyer. Parents do have the right to apply for legal aid for lawyers to help them prepare for the tribunal hearing, but cannot ask for legal aid to cover the costs of a lawyer attending the hearing itself. The rules for legal aid are rigorous, so it is likely that the majority of parents would be ineligible for this assistance. Legal aid cannot be applied for on behalf of the child, as the child is not a party to the appeal.

Lodging an appeal

The local education authority should make available to the parents information about the appeal process. They should provide, either on request, or with the notice of their decision against which the parents may appeal, a copy of a leaflet entitled: 'Special Educational Needs Tribunal – How to appeal'. This leaflet contains the form on which the parents can write out the details of their appeal. Many voluntary organisations also hold copies of this leaflet.

Some education authorities are informing parents of their rights to appeal, but not enclosing the tribunal leaflet. Instead they are indicating that the forms are available from the authority. Parents who already feel they are in conflict with the authority may be reluctant to contact the officer to ask for an appeal leaflet; further, they may resent the fact that the authority appears to be making appeal difficult. Other professionals involved with parents in the identification and assessment of their child's needs should have a copy of the leaflet available to show to parents who may ask for information. The leaflet contains details of where more copies can be obtained (also, see Appendix C).

Preparing for appeal

The appeal process is designed to take around four months, from lodging an appeal to the appeal hearing being held. After the parents have lodged their appeal, the tribunal will write to the local education authority informing them of the fact and asking for an initial response. This leads to an exchange of correspondence that may clarify the argument to such an extent that an agreement can be reached without the appeal hearing taking place. This is likely to happen in only a minority of cases.

During the four-month period, parents need to gather together all the evidence and information they have that supports their case, and may gather additional evidence from specialists that can add more weight to their argument. Clearly the local education authority also has the right to do this.

The tribunal has the right to ask for documents to be disclosed during the appeal process and at the hearing; this may include documents in internal files that relate to the child but have not previously been disclosed to the parents.

By the time the appeal hearing is held, both the parents and the education authority should have been able to see all the evidence from both parties.

At the appeal

Parents may take along to the hearing up to two 'expert witnesses', who are likely to be professionals such as psychologists, or therapists, or educationalists. Although the tribunal reimburses the expenses for expert witnesses to attend the hearing, the parents may have to pay their witnesses for their time in both preparing for and attending the hearing. Parents may also take a 'friend' who may be their 'Named Person', and this can be in addition to any representative (e.g., lawyer) whom they have engaged.

The child may also attend the tribunal hearing, but is not a party to the proceedings. These are between the parents and the authority, not between the child and the authority. If the child attends the hearing, and he or she is considered to have sufficient understanding, the tribunal may ask the child to express his or her own views. The child may also make a written statement. If the child is taken along to participate in the hearing, this will count as one of the parents' two possible witnesses.

What is important is that any professional involved in a case where the parent is lodging an appeal should be able to advise the parent of the possible difficulties, and support them through the process. At the very least, the stress and anxiety of preparing an appeal will show as the hearing approaches, and teachers and others need to be aware of this and take it into account in dealing with the parents throughout this period, whether or not their dealings are directly related to the appeal itself.

Other routes of complaint

As with the system prior to the 1993 Education Act, parents still have the right to complain to the Secretary of State, or to the Ombudsman, or take a case to Judicial Review.

Judicial Review is used where the local education authority may have acted illegally.

The Ombudsman is used where the local authority may be guilty of maladministration – for example by failing to follow its own procedures.

Parents may complain to the Secretary of State if all other school- and authority-based procedures have failed to resolve a complaint, and the complaint is based on the school or education authority failing to carry out their duties or acting unreasonably. Complaint to the Secretary of State is directed to the Secretary of State for Education in England, at the Department for Education; in Wales, parents should write to the Secretary of State for Wales at the Welsh Office Education Department.

The best strategy for dealing with complaints is to prevent them. This is done not by suppressing them, but by developing systems and procedures for parents to express their views at all appropriate opportunities, so that they can raise concerns as early and as openly as possible. The most effective strategy is to develop partnership with parents, on an individual basis, school basis, and authority basis; through developing links with local and national voluntary organisations and parent support groups; and by using some or all of the strategies outlined in this book.

Appendix A: Parental survey

Between January and March 1995, a survey was conducted among approximately 100 families from all over England and Wales, who had children with special educational needs; a wide range of special needs were identified, of varying severity. The aim was to identify common themes among parents regarding their perceptions of how staff in schools and LEAs dealt with them and their children. It also looked at the involvement of health agencies. The following is a brief summary of the results of this survey. It is not presented as being statistically representative of the SEN population as a whole, as families have been self-selecting. There is in particular a larger than standard proportion of children with dyspraxia or motor co-ordination difficulties. However, the responses do reflect common themes, irrespective of the child's disability or special need, and these are reported here.

Age of child (at time of survey)	%
Pre-school	10
5–11	62
12–16	25
16+	3

Years since difficulties first recognised/suspected:	%
<5	38
5–10	44
>10	18

	%
Children with Statements:	72

Type of SEN	*(% of children presenting)*
Dyslexia/literacy problems	21
General learning difficulties	15
Developmental delay	7
Speech and/or language difficulties	27
Moderate learning difficulties	3
Cerebral palsy/physical impairment	6
Down's syndrome	10
Dyspraxia/co-ordination difficulties	25
Emotional/behavioural difficulties	7
Autism/communication difficulties	10
Visual impairment	1
Hearing impairment	6
Severe learning difficulties	3
Other medical	6

% with more than one type of SEN	38
Both parents able to be involved in decisions	98
Other family members involved in making decisions	17

Experience with school staff in identifying/supporting the SEN

SENCOs were more usually seen as having special training and being more open about a child's SEN. They are generally seen as helpful and easy to talk with.

Teachers and head teachers fall into two groups: those who are helpful and those who are not. Helpfulness is not directly correlated to experience of the child's particular type of difficulty, neither is it a function of specialist SEN training. Many teachers were new to a particular difficulty, but still worked hard to understand and meet the child's needs. Specialist staff in special schools and units were generally seen as helpful, although this was not always the case.

For children undergoing assessment, or who had recently undergone assessment, only a small proportion of parents indicated that the teachers, head teachers or SENCOs had been helpful during the assessment process. In only a minority of cases did the parents believe that the school staff understood the assessment process.

Once a Statement had been drafted, only a minority of schools discussed its implementation with the parents, and this was often at the parents' instigation. The responsibility for the discussion fell equally between class teacher, SENCO and head teacher.

Very few parents knew or believed that their child's teacher or teachers had read or understood their child's Statement.

Educational psychologists

More parents were satisfied than dissatisfied with the way the educational psychologist dealt with their child's assessments and subsequent discussions with parents. The items indicating satisfaction included: willingness by the educational psychologist to listen to the parents' own views; sight of any reports written, before they were sent to the school/LEA; psychologist's availability for follow-up discussions; and confidence that he or she understands the child's difficulties. Many parents were unsure whether the psychologist had talked to the school to offer advice or useful suggestions.

Advisory teachers

Where an advisory teacher had been involved – for the most part, pre-school – more parents expressed confidence and satisfaction than not. Again, there was some doubt as to whether the advisory teacher had

150

discussed the child's needs with the school, but given that most were pre-school advisory teachers, this is not significant.

Designated medical officers

Most parents felt that the medical officer was willing to listen to their own views. However, they were often felt not to involve themselves in discussions with the school, and were often not available for follow-up discussions on the advice they submitted for statutory assessments.

Named Officers

Many parents whose children had a Statement were not aware of who the Named Officer was, or that they had one. More parents felt that the officer was unwilling to listen to their views than felt they were willing. There was almost a direct correlation between the officer's willingness to listen to parental views and parents' belief that the officer understood their child's SEN.

Information about assessment procedures

The professional who most frequently provided information about the procedures for assessment was the educational psychologist. The second most frequent information provider was the designated medical officer. Named Officers came third, closely followed by advisory teachers (but this might reflect the lower frequency of involvement by this group). Named Officers often only provided information in writing, and this was described as 'brief'. In around 10 per cent of cases, none of the professionals explained the procedures.

Involvement of medical professionals

Parents were asked to identify which medical professionals had been involved with their child over the time that the special needs were identified and assessed. A list was provided which included speech and language therapist, physiotherapist, occupational therapist, developmental paediatrician, audiologist, ophthalmologist, neurologist, clinical psychologist, psychiatrist, GP, health visitor and 'other' (to be specified).

- 9 per cent indicated no additional medical specialists
- 4 per cent indicated one
- 6 per cent indicated two
- 12 per cent indicated three
- 15 per cent indicated four
- 12 per cent indicated five
- 12 per cent indicated six
- 15 per cent indicated seven
- 6 per cent indicated eight
- 3 per cent indicated each of nine, ten and eleven additional medical specialists.

Appropriate advice sought

As many as 23 per cent of parents felt that some key specialist had been left out when the medical advice was gathered and submitted to the LEA. In some cases, these were key individuals, such as developmental paediatricians in cases of children with motor developmental or co-ordination difficulties; occupational therapists for children with motor co-ordination difficulties; hearing clinics and audiologists for children with Down's syndrome; specialist language therapists for children with speech and language difficulties; a speech therapist for a child with profound hearing loss; and specialists retained privately by the parents, such as a physiotherapist and speech therapist for a child with cerebral palsy. In several cases, parents indicated that they, and not the designated medical officer, had acted as co-ordinator of all the medical reports.

Use of independent/private specialists

More than half of the parents indicated that they had sought independent advice, either through the NHS (from specialist centres for medical advice) or by private commission (most frequently for educational psychology, speech and language and occupational therapies).

In the majority of cases, the independent/private advice differed in content, although not necessarily in conclusions, from that provided 'through the system'. Differences were resolved for the most part by discussion or exchanges of correspondence, often resulting in the LEA giving preference to the independent advice.

In the vast majority of cases, parents considered the quality of the advice received independently to be superior, even where the conclusions and advice did not differ. Parents noted particularly that the information acquired independently was more detailed, offered more opportunities for discussion and explanation, and reflected a better understanding of the individual child.

Parental contribution to assessment

Most parents said they had sent their own views on their child's SEN to the LEA. Of the few who had not done this, the reasons were: they had not recognized the point at which they were asked to do so; they wanted to see what the LEA said first; they were not given information on what to say.

Of those that did make a contribution, the majority received help from a variety of sources, including: a leaflet from the LEA 26 per cent; the school 10 per cent; the educational psychologist 6 per cent; a friend 12 per cent; a voluntary organisation 46 per cent.

Of those who did not receive any help, about a third did not know where to go for help; the remainder indicated that they did not think they needed any.

Annual reviews

One third of parents whose children had had Statements for more than a year had not attended an annual review each year.

Of those parents who did attend reviews, one third did not feel that their views were taken into account during the reviews. Not surprisingly, most of these parents were unhappy with the outcome of the reviews. In addition, about a third of those whose views had been 'taken into account' were unhappy with the review outcome.

16+ options

Only a small proportion of parents were in the position of having to consider post-16 options. Those that were, however, expressed concern about the future. There was a general lack of confidence about where to go for information.

Concern was expressed by parents of children as young as eleven and twelve years of age, and including parents of children who did not have a Statement.

Appendix B: Writing about your child – notes for parents[1]

Very few of us ever have to write in detail about our children. It is difficult, and can often be painful – remembering difficulties and problems alongside hopes and expectations. But you know your child better than anyone else – and your views count when other 'experts' are examining your child and making decisions about his or her future.

These notes are intended for guidance, to help you begin to write about your child, so that your views can be included in assessments and Statements about your child's special educational needs.

Some headings may not apply to you (for example, when writing about a much older child you will not necessarily need to cover crawling, drawing, etc., but might want to discuss subjects he/she is good at or enjoys), and there may be things you want to say which don't fit into any of these headings.

You might find that you end up writing a great deal: once you have your thoughts down on paper, see if you can make it simpler. But don't lose anything which you feel is important.

The early years

- What do you remember about the early months/years? (If you have other children, you might like to consider how they were different, and how they were the same, at comparable ages.)
- Was there anything specific about his/her birth and very early development which caused concern?
- Were you happy with your child's progress as a baby/toddler: were any particular concerns raised by you, or the baby clinic, or health visitor, or anyone else at that time?
- When did you first feel or notice that something might not be quite right? Who did you seek advice from? What advice were you given? Did that make a difference? Was there an improvement, or did things get worse?

---

[1]These guidelines are built upon those initially developed by Sheila Wolfendale in 1983/4, which have provided the basis for many similar guidelines, including those incorporated in the Code of Practice.

What is your child like now?

(For each one of these, try also to think when he/she first achieved any of these skills, or if a skill/ability was once there and has since been lost, or if there are any factors which have caused an improvement or worsening of these abilities.)

- *General health:* eating and sleeping habits; general fitness; minor ailments; causes of absences from school (frequent/occasional, a few days/prolonged periods); recent periods in hospital; current medicines, special diet or other therapies (e.g., physiotherapy, occupational therapy).
- *Physical skills:* can he/she crawl, walk, jump, climb stairs, ride a bike, catch a ball, build with bricks, do jigsaws, scribble, draw, write, sew, cut things out with scissors?
- *Self-help skills:* dressing, undressing (zips, buttons, shoelaces, pull-ons, etc.); feeding (including knife, fork, spoon, straw, ordinary cup); toileting (*how much* help is needed); brushing/combing hair, washing hands and face, wiping nose, etc.
- *Communication:* does he/she point, make gestures, copy sounds, use single words, phrases or complete sentences? (can anyone understand, or only parents/teachers and close friends?); does he/she understand and respond to others? (anyone, or only parent/teacher or close friend?); does he/she start conversations or only answer when spoken to?; can he/she tell you what has happened (e.g. at school, or while you were out of the house)?; can he/she describe other people or events?
- *Playing and learning at home:* what are his/her favourite toys and activities, and have these changed over the months/years?; can he/she concentrate on any activity, or only some?; does he/she play alone or with others, and if with others, is it sharing and co-operative play?; what games/stories or TV programmes does he/she enjoy?
- *Activities outside home:* what playgroups or other activity groups does he/she attend?; how does he/she cope with being separated from parent/carer?; has this changed?
- *Relationships:* how does he/she get on with parents, carers, brother(s), sister(s), other relatives, neighbours, family friends, either when they visit at home, or when contact is made 'outside'? Does he/she mix well or remain alone in a group?
- *Behaviour:* does he/she co-operate with instructions, share, listen? How has this changed? (You might find it helpful to describe how a particular task is achieved now, and how he/she learned to obey.) Does he/she understand and co-operate with family 'rules'? Does

he/she have mood swings, sulking or temper tantrums: is he/she affectionate, easily upset? How easily does he/she get over an upset? How excitable is he/she, for example, in anticipation of Christmas, birthday, family outing, etc.?

- *At school:* relationships with other children and teachers, and other carers. Progress with reading, writing, numbers, constructive activities, drawing, painting, classroom activities. How has the school helped or not helped (either formal teaching, or general way of life, or other staff such as dinner ladies, welfare helpers, etc.)? Does he/she enjoy school? Is he/she being stretched to achieve his/her abilities? (It is particularly helpful if your child has been to more than one school, or has had more than one teacher, to try to compare how he/she achieved at each, and what you think made the difference.)

Your general views

- How do you compare your child with others of the same age? Or with brothers/sisters? Or with your own expectations?
- What is your child good at? What does your child enjoy doing?
- What does he/she worry about: is he/she aware of his/her own difficulties?

Other people's views

- Have you had any reports from doctors, psychologists or other experts which you find helpful? (If necessary, add copies of the reports at the end of your letter, and refer to them in this part of the letter.)

The future

- What do you think your child's special educational needs are?
- What sort of things are most likely to help (particular equipment, teaching styles, level of adult support, size of class, types of children in group/class, level of home/school links)?
- Are there a mixture of educational and social needs which might be better served by: very local school to help him/her make friends at home?; residential school where links between school day and out-of-school-hours are 'built in'?; maximum home contact, or reduced home contact? (e.g., if boarding, weekly or termly?)
- What other considerations are there? (any particular family

circumstances: access to transport, other children in the family, etc.)

- Is there anyone else who you think should be consulted about your child's assessment, who isn't already on the list of experts? (The LEA will already ask the head teacher of your child's current school, the educational psychologist who works with that school, and either your own consultant paediatrician, or their medical officer, who can call for information from your GP: they may also ask the social services, if this might be relevant.)

Note: although the head teacher, educational psychologists, paediatrician and GP will each be making a report, you should talk in detail with them about their thoughts on your child. You may be able to explain some things to them (e.g., about his/her behaviour or family circumstances, or your concerns), and if they have misunderstood something about your child's abilities, behaviour or skills, you should have a chance to discuss this before they make their reports. It is also worth checking with them to find out who else they will be asking for information.

Summary

- Try to pull all these thoughts into a short summary: a few sentences on the sort of school, style of teaching, subjects, equipment you think are required; and a few sentences on your expectations of what your child could achieve as a result.

Appendix C – Useful contacts

This appendix lists some of the main organisations that offer services to parents and/or professionals, including help, information, advice, equipment and training. Inclusion in this list does not imply recommendation: readers are encouraged to evaluate the appropriateness of the services of each organisation according to their own requirements.

Many of the organisations listed here are registered charities, and they are often run by volunteers on very limited budgets. If making enquiries in writing, please enclose an SAE wherever possible.

ACE – see Advisory Centre for Education
Action for Special Educational Needs – ASpEN
Dunsley Orchard
London Road
Tring
Hertfordshire
HP23 6HA
Tel/Fax: 01442 82 3765
Parent support group offering help across all types of SEN and all stages of Code of Practice, specifically in Hertfordshire, Bedfordshire and Buckinghamshire, with some help available further afield.

Advisory Centre for Education (ACE) Ltd
1b Aberdeen Studios
22–4 Highbury Grove
London
N5 2EA
Tel: 0171 354 8321
Telephone helpline (2–5 pm weekdays) for advice on all aspects of education law, including SEN. Wide range of publications available.

AFASIC (Overcoming Speech Impairments)
347 Central Market
Smithfield
London
EC1A 9NH
Tel: 0171 236 3632
Support and information for parents and professionals regarding speech and language difficulties: local branches.

ASBAH – see Association for Spina Bifida and Hydrocephalus

ASpEN – see Action for Special Educational Needs

Association for Brain-Damaged Children and Young Adults
Clifton House
3 St Paul's Road
Foleshill
Coventry
CV6 5DE
Tel: 01203 665 450
Local charity in city of Coventry.

Association for Spina Bifida and Hydrocephalus (ASBAH)
42 Park Road
Peterborough
Cambridgeshire
PE1 2UQ
Tel: 01733 555 988
Fax: 01733 555 985
Advice and support for parents and professionals. Local branches. Contact Peter Walker, Education Adviser.

158

Association for the Education and Welfare of the Visually Handicapped (VIEW)
Lyon House
Exhall Grange Special School
Wheelwright Lane
Ash Green
Coventry
CV7 9HP
Tel: 01203 361 127
Fax: 01203 645 074
   VIEW is a registered charity concerned with the education and welfare of visually-impaired people. It is a membership organisation open to visually-impaired individuals, parents, professionals and others working in the field of visual impairment.

Association of National Specialist Colleges (NATSPEC)
c/o Lord Mayor Treloar College
Holybourne
Alton
Hants
GU34 4EN
Tel: 01420 547 400
Fax: 01420 542 708

Barnado's
Tanners Lane
Barkingside
Ilford
Essex
IG6 1QS
Tel: 0181 550 8822
   Runs community projects in deprived areas, disability support services, fostering and adoption services.

BATOD – see British Association of Teachers of the Deaf

BDA – see British Dyslexia Association

BILD – see British Institute of Learning Difficulties

BIRD – see Centre for Brain Injury Rehabilitation and Development

British Association of Teachers of the Deaf (BATOD)
41 The Orchard
Leven
Beverley
N Humberside
HU17 5QA
Tel/Fax/Minicom: 01964 544 243
   Area and national meetings to promote the education of hearing-impaired children and protect the interests of teachers of the deaf.

British Deaf Association
38 Victoria Place
Carlisle
CA1 1HU
Tel: 01228 48844
   Advances and promotes the interests of deaf people.

British Dyslexia Association (BDA)
98 London Road
Reading
Berkshire
RG1 5AU
Tel: 0173 4668 271
Fax: 0173 4351 927
   National charity with 100 local associations.

British Epilepsy Association
Anstey House
40 Hanover Square
Leeds
LS3 1BE
Tel: 01132 439 393
Fax: 01132 428 804
  Advice and information for parents and professionals.

British Institute for Brain Injured Children
Knowle Hall
Bridgwater
Somerset
TA7 8PJ
Tel: 01278 684 060
Fax: 01278 685 573
  Parent information and support: assessments, therapy programmes.

British Institute of Learning Disabilities (BILD)
Wolverhampton Road
Kidderminster
Worcestershire
DY10 3PP
Tel: 01562 850 251
Fax: 01562 851 970
  Support, advice and information for professionals.

British Psychological Society
48 Princes Road East
Leicester
LE1 7DR
Tel: 01162 549 568
Fax: 01162 470 787
  Professional association.

CDC – see Council for Disabled Children

Centre for Brain Injury Rehabilitation and Development (BIRD)
131 Main Road
Broughton
Chester
Cheshire
CH4 0NR
Tel: 01244 532 047
Fax: 01244 538 723
  Provides assessment, treatment and therapy for children with physical and/or learning disability.

Centre for Studies on Integration in Education (CSIE)
415 Edgware Road
London
NW2 6NB
Tel: 0181 452 8642
  Advice for parents and professionals on supporting SEN in mainstream.

Child Psychotherapy Trust
21 Maresfield Gardens
London
NW3 5SH
Tel: 0171 433 3867
Fax: 0171 433 1874
  National charity dedicated to increasing the number of child psychotherapists available throughout the UK to treat emotionally-damaged children, adolescents and their families.

College of Speech and Language Therapists
7 Bath Place
Rivington Street
London
EC2A 3DR
Tel: 0171 613 3855
Fax: 0171 613 3854
Professional association.

Contact-a-Family
170 Tottenham Court Road
London
W1P 0HA
Tel: 0171 383 3555
Fax: 0171 383 0259
Co-ordinates a network of 800 local support groups for parents of children with special needs. Also works with 300 national support groups for children's specific conditions, many of which are rare syndromes. Aims to link families together for mutual support.

Council for Disabled Children – CDC
8 Wakley Street
London
EC1V 7QE
Tel: 0171 843 6000
Fax: 0171 278 9512
Information about services and sources of help.

CSIE – see Centre for Studies on Integration in Education

Cystic Fibrosis Research Trust
Alexandra House
5 Blyth Road
Bromley
Kent
BR1 3RS
Tel: 0181 464 7211
Fax: 0181 313 0472
The CF Trust provides support and advice to families who have a child with CF and to the growing numbers of adults with CF. There is a network of trained volunteer support workers who can be contacted through the Family and Adult Support Services Department.

Department for Education
Sanctuary Buildings
Great Smith Street
Westminster
London
SW1P 3BT
Tel: 0171 925 5000
Fax: 0171 925 6000

Department for Education Publications Despatch
PO Box 6927
London
E3 3NZ
Tel: 0171 510 0150
Fax: 0171 510 0196
For copies of the Parents' Charter and the SEN tribunal leaflet.

Department for Education – special needs publications
Tel: 01787 880 946
For copies of the Code of Practice or parents' guide to SEN.

DIAL – see Disablement Information and Advice Line

Disability Law Service
Room 241
49–51 Bedford Row
London
WC1R 4LR
Tel: 0171 831 7740
Free legal advice and assistance regarding education and other issues for disabled people, their families and carers/enablers.

Disablement Information and Advice Line (DIAL)
Park Lodge
St Catherine's Hospital
Tickhill Road
Balby
Doncaster
Yorks
DN4 8QN
Tel: 01302 310 123
Over 100 local centres in the UK, run by disabled people, and offering advice on all aspects of disability.

Down's Syndrome Association
153-5 Mitcham Road
London
SW17 9PG
Tel: 0181 682 4001
Information and advice for parents, carers and professionals.

Dyslexia Institute
133 Gresham Road
Staines
Middlesex
TW18 2AJ
Tel: 01784 463 851
Fax: 01784 460 747

Dyspraxia Trust
PO Box 30
Hitchin
Herts
SG5 1UU
Tel: 01462 454 986
Support, information and advice, for parents and professionals, regarding children who have dyspraxia (also known as minimal brain dysfunction, clumsy child syndrome, etc.)

Foundation for Conductive Education
6th Floor
Clathorpe House
30 Hagley Road
Edgbaston
Birmingham
B16 8QY
Tel: 0121 456 5533
Fax: 0121 456 5792
Has established Conductive Education [a system for children and adults with motor disorders] in the UK.

Helen Arkell Dyslexia Centre
Frensham
Farnham
Surrey
GU10 3BW
Tel: 01252 792 400
Support for children with specific learning difficulty: assessment, tuition, speech and language therapy, short courses: also teacher training, support for schools.

Hornsey Centre for Children with Cerebral Palsy
26a Dukes Avenue
London
N10 2PT
Tel: 0181 444 7242
Fax: 0181 444 7241
 Provides education based on conductive education.

ICAN – see Invalid Children's Aid Nationwide

Independent Panel for Special Education Advice (IPSEA)
22 Warren Hill Road
Woodbridge
Suffolk
IP12 4DU
Tel: 01394 382 814
 Helps provide second opinions regarding professional advice: provides advice on Statementing.

Institute for Neurophysiological Psychology
4 Stanley Place
Chester
Cheshire
CH1 2LU
Tel: 01244 311 414
 Research and information regarding CNS [central nervous system] dysfunction and its relationship with learning difficulties, and devising treatment programmes.

In Touch
Ann Worthington MBE
10 Norman Road
Sale
Cheshire
M33 3DF
Tel: 0161 905 2440
 Contact and information services for parents of children with any type of special needs, especially rare disorders.

Invalid Children's Aid Nationwide (ICAN)
Barbican City Gate
1-3 Dufferin Street
London
EC1Y 8NA
Tel: 0171 374 4422
Fax: 0171 374 2762
 ICAN is a national charity for children with special educational needs. At present a large part of ICAN's work is with children who have speech and language difficulties. ICAN is the leading specialist in this field and runs three schools and two nurseries for children with these difficulties. ICAN also runs the only national school for children with asthma and eczema.

IPSEA – see Independent Panel for Special Education Advice

LADDER (Attention Deficit (and Hyperactivity) Disorder)
142 Mostyn Road
London
SW19 3LR
Tel: 0181 543 2800
Fax: 0181 543 4800
 Support and information for parents of children with attention deficit disorder (ADD) or attention deficit hyperactivity disorder (ADHD). Can also provide INSET, training and consultancy for professionals and other groups. Publications list available.

Learning Development Aids
Duke Street
Wisbech
Cambridgeshire

PE13 2AE
Tel: 01945 53441
Fax: 01945 587361

LOOK
Miss Anne Marie Kelly
Administrative Assistant
Queen Alexandra College
49 Court Oak Road
Birmingham
B17 9TG
Tel: 0121 428 5038
Fax: 0121 428 5048
  Federation of groups concerned with visual impairment in children.

MENCAP (Royal Society for Mentally Handicapped Children and Adults)
123 Golden Lane
London
EC1Y 0RT
Tel: 0171 454 0454
  Support and advice for parents and carers. Regional offices and local societies.

MIND (National Association for Mental Health)
Granta House
15-19 Broadway
London
E15 4BQ
Tel: 0181 519 2122

NASEN – see National Association for Special Educational Needs

National Association for Gifted Children
Park Campus
Boughton Green Road
Northampton
NN2 7AL
Tel: 01604 792 300
  Information and advice for parents and professionals: INSET services for schools.

National Association for Special Educational Needs (NASEN)
York House
Exhall Grange
Wheelwright Lane
Coventry
CV7 9HP
Tel/Fax (Membership): 01203 362 414
Tel (Publications): 01785 46872
Fax (Publications): 01785 41187
  Backed by a high level of expertise, NASEN exists to promote the development of children and young people with special educational needs, wherever they are located, and to support those who work with them. NASEN publishes two quarterly journals, *Support for Learning* and *British Journal of Special Education,* and a termly magazine, *Special.* Through its trading company, NASEN Enterprises Ltd, it publishes a range of practical publications and organises courses. UK membership is concentrated in a network of over seventy branches.

National Autistic Society
276 Willesden Lane
London
NW2 5RB
Tel: 0181 451 1114
Fax: 0181 451 5865
  Information, advice and support for parents, families and carers of people with autism and Asperger syndrome.

National Deaf Children's Society (NDCS)
15 Dufferin Street
London
EC1Y 8PD
Tel: 0171 250 0123 (voice and text)
Fax: 0171 251 5020
   Co-ordinates policy development and publications. Support advice and information for families and professionals. Advice on technology for hearing-impaired children.

National Library for the Handicapped Child
Reach Resource Centre
Wellington House
Wellington Road
Wokingham
Berkshire
RG11 2AG
Tel: 01734 891 101
Fax: 01734 790 989
   Collection of books, audio-visual aids, etc., on all aspects of special needs in children. Resource and information centre for parents, students, teachers, etc., concerned with children whose disability or learning problems affect their ability to read.

NATSPEC – see Association of National Specialist Colleges

NDCS – see National Deaf Children's Society

Network 81
Chapel Hill
Stansted
Essex
CM24 8AJ
Tel: 01279 647 415
Fax: 01279 816 438
   National network of parents of children with SEN. Local branches.

Paget-Gorman Signed Speech (PGSS)
3 Gipsy Lane
Headington
Oxford
OX3 7PT
Tel: 01865 61908
   Helps speech- and language-disordered children to communicate. Offers advice and information for parents and professionals, publications and training courses.

Parents in Partnership
Unit 2
Ground Floor
70 South Lambeth Road
London
SW8 1RL
Tel: 0171 735 7735
Fax: 0171 735 3828
   Parents' support organisation offering information and assistance to parents and others with an interest in SEN.

PGSS – see Paget-Gorman Signed Speech

Rathbone Society
1st Floor
The Excalibur Building
77 Whitworth Street
Manchester
M1 6EZ
Tel: 0161 236 5358
Fax: 0161 236 4539
   National society working for people with learning difficulties.

RNIB – see Royal National Institute for the Blind

RNID – see Royal National Institute for the Deaf

Royal National Institute for the Blind (RNIB)
224 Great Portland Street
London
W1N 6AA
Tel: 0171 388 1266
Fax: 0171 383 4921
    The RNIB supports blind and partially-sighted children in special and mainstream schools. They run six special schools, five of them for children with multiple disabilities. Through a national network of education centres, they support children in local schools by training teachers and providing equipment and specialist expertise.

Royal National Institute for the Deaf (RNID)
105 Gower Street
London
WC1E 6AH
Tel: 0171 387 8033
Fax: 0171 388 2346

SCOPE (formerly the Spastics Society)
Education Services
16 Fitzroy Square
London
W1P 5HQ
Tel: 0171 387 9571
    Offers information and advice: also multidisciplinary assessment service.

SENNAC – see Special Educational Needs National Advisory Council

SENSE – the National Deaf-Blind and Rubella Association
113 Clifton Terrace
Finsbury Park
London
N4 3SR
Tel: 0171 272 7774
Fax: 0171 272 6012

SNAP – see Special Needs Advisory Project

Spastics Society – see SCOPE

Special Educational Needs National Advisory Council (SENNAC)
Hillside
271 Woolton Road
Liverpool
Tel: 0151 722 3819
Fax: 0151 794 2512

Special Needs Advisory Project
3 Links Court
Fortran Road
St Mellons
Cardiff
CF3 0SP
Tel: 01222 362143
    Parent support network for Mid, South and West Glamorgan, Gwent, Dyfed and Gwynedd.

VIEW – see Association for the Education and Welfare of the Visually Handicapped

Bibliography

Department for Education publications (all 1994, London)

Code of Practice on the identification and assessment of special educational needs.
Education (Special Educational Needs) Regulations, The.
Education (Special Educational Needs) (Information) Regulations, The.
Special educational needs – a guide for parents.
Special Educational Needs Tribunal – How to appeal.

Other publications:

Education Act, 1993, HMSO, London.
Leonard, Anne, *Right from the Start,* 1994, SCOPE (formerly the Spastics Society), London; ISBN 0 946828 38 5.

Index